100
BEST
VEGETARIAN
RECIPES

CAROL GELLES

WILEY

John Wiley & Sons, Inc.

Copyright © 2008 Carol Gelles

Published by John Wiley & Sons, Inc., Hoboken, New Jersey

Published simultaneously in Canada

Gelles, Carol.
100 best vegetarian recipes/Carol Gelles.
p. cm.
Includes index.
ISBN 978-0-470-18550-6 (cloth)
1. Vegetarian cookery. I. Title.
TX837.G386 2008
641.5'636—dc22

2007024687

Printed in China

10 9 8 7 6 5 4 3 2 1

Portions of this work have been previously published in *1,000 Vegetarian Recipes* (Wiley, 1996).

Interior Photos: Sang An, p.97; E. Jane Armstrong, p.69; Mary Ellen Bartley, p.73; David Bishop, p.33; John Blais, p.95; Rob Fiocca, p.77; Dana Gallagher, pp.89, 123; Sheri Giblin, p.55; Alexandra Grablewski, p.53; Brian Hagiwara, pp.111, 141; Richard Jung, p.25; Jennifer Levy, p.127; Pornchai Mittongtare, p.41; David Prince, p.149; Erik Rank, pp.65, 75; Lew Robertson, p.29; David Roth, p.103; Stock-Yard Studio, p.93; Ann Stratton, p.61; Mark Thomas, pp.49, 79, 101, 113; Luca Trovato, p.51; Elizabeth Watt, p.45; Jonelle Weaver, p.153. All Photos from Food Pix/Jupiter Images.

CONTENTS

ACKNOWLEDGMENTS

As with any project, there are many people who make it happen. This book was the idea of my editor Linda Ingroia and she participated in every step of the project. Her assistant Charleen Barila also added her thoughts and suggestions. As ever, my agent Judith Weber was my adviser, advocate, and friend. I know I will never meet the countless others who worked on this book throughout the publishing process, but I thank them all. Speaking of people I have never met, I want to thank my readers. I thank all the people who have loved *1,000 Vegetarian Recipes*. For without you, there would be no need for a "Best of..." book. Finally, I thank all my friends and family for their support through this project, all the "careers du jour," and the ups and downs that life presents. I count each and every one of you as a blessing.

AUTHOR'S NOTE

Writing *1,000 Vegetarian Recipes*, a book that won two awards, was a daunting assignment; choosing my favorite recipes from it, on the other hand, was a total pleasure. The recipes I've chosen for this book work for everyday meals or for special occasion menus and will please both vegetarians and meat-eaters. I offer a range of flavors and ethnic cuisines, as well as a variety of cooking styles. There are enough recipes and information in this book to find any vegetarian staple as well as recipes that will inspire you, and enough scope that you will never have to turn elsewhere.

This book contains classic recipes, as well as many variations to appeal to diverse tastes. I urge you to read the recipes' headnotes and variations because they contain many extra ideas and cooking tips. The introduction, sidebars, and *Basics* chapter contain information on how the recipes work, important cooking tables, what you need to keep on hand, how to be a healthy vegetarian, and how to plan a meal or event, along with some menus to get you started. It is my sincere hope you will enjoy using this book as much as I enjoyed putting it together for you.

Bon appétit!

BEING A VEGETARIAN

A vegetarian, by definition, is a person who does not eat the flesh of anything that was previously living. Some vegetarians are willing to use animal products as long as the animal was not harmed in the process. Others go a step further and eschew using any animal products at all, including honey, wool, leather, fur, etc.

PESCO-LACTO-OVO Technically not vegetarians, because while they do not eat meat, they do eat fish, eggs, and dairy products.

LACTO-OVO Do not eat meat, but do eat eggs and dairy products.

LACTO Do not eat meat or eggs, but do eat dairy products.

OVO Do not eat meat or dairy products but do eat eggs.

VEGAN or STRICT VEGETARIAN Do not eat meat, dairy products, or eggs, and may or may not eat animal by-products.

People who are vegetarians for religious reasons usually have the support of their family, as everyone follows the same dietary guidelines of their religion. However, some vegetarians may face certain obstacles, such as being the only vegetarians in their families. In this scenario, the best defense is a good offense.

• Learn to cook! Prepare your own vegetarian meals for yourself or for family and friends.

• Pack your own lunches.

• Volunteer to bring a dish when invited to someone's home for dinner.

• When eating out, try ethnic cuisines such as Italian, Mexican, Indian, and Chinese. Their menus are filled with appealing vegetarian specialties.

As more and more people become vegetarians, the world is becoming more vegetarian-friendly. You will find it a satisfying way of life.

VEGETARIANISM AND HEALTH

It's easy to miss out on many important nutrients when you follow a fast-food lifestyle. By switching to a vegetarian diet—one that is based on vegetables, fruits, grains, and beans—you'll find yourself easily meeting the recommended five (or more) servings of fruits and vegetables per day. Variety ensures that you will get the wide range of vitamins, minerals, and fiber you need.

Cholesterol was once considered the major dietary villain in heart disease, but avoiding saturated fats and reducing total fat intake is also important in a heart-healthy diet. Avoid saturated fats like butter and tropical oils.

Polyunsaturated fats are oils made from plant sources; canola and safflower oils are particularly healthy choices, although any vegetable oil is fine. Olive oil is monounsaturated, and current scientific findings show this to be the healthiest oil of all.

The simple truth is there is no cholesterol in any vegetable, fruit, nut, grain, or bean. Cholesterol is found only in animal products. Strict vegetarians (vegans) have automatically eliminated all cholesterol from their diet. Lacto-ovo vegetarians should remember that eggs, butter, and cheese are animal products and you will still have to watch out for cholesterol (and fat). You can reduce your cholesterol and fat by incorporating some healthy substitutions to your diet:

• Use extra egg whites in place of the yolk (two egg whites equal one whole egg).

• Look for low-fat or nonfat varieties of cheese.

• Select low-fat or nonfat dairy products instead of those containing whole milk.

THE RECIPES

My approach to recipe development is one of moderation, and I've tried to balance flavor with health considerations.

If you are on a very low-fat diet, many of these recipes will still contain too much fat for you; however, in recipes with sautéed ingredients you can reduce the fat content by half if you cook in a nonstick skillet. (Note: I chose to test these recipes with common household equipment, rather than specialized items such as nonstick skillets.)

Similarly, these recipes may be too salty for people who are limiting their sodium intake. You can easily just omit salt wherever called for and be sure to buy salt-free bouillon or make homemade salt-free broth (page 158).

I've included both the yield and the number of servings because the number of people each recipe will serve may vary depending on your menu. Consider your audience: if your household consists of 2 adults and 2 teenage sons, a lasagna may only serve 4 to 6 people. You probably know how many people in your family 3 cups of rice will serve—it may be more or less than the number I have suggested.

I have intentionally prepared some recipes in large batches because I believe it's nice to have leftovers to use in the next day or two or freeze for the future. You'll find this to be especially true in the soup chapter. I also include some larger-yield recipes to allow for company. If you are not fond of leftovers, just check the yield before you choose a recipe.

This book contains enough egg- and dairy-free recipes to be useful for all kinds of vegetarians, including vegans. Each recipe is marked with an icon that indicates the type of vegetarian it is suited for. There is also a code identifying recipes that can be prepared in advance of serving time:

LO = Lacto-Ovo

L = Lacto

V = Vegan

✳ = Vegan Variation (a variation suitable for vegans described below the main recipe)

M = Make-Ahead (can be prepared ahead of serving time)

A FEW INGREDIENT NOTES

DAIRY PRODUCTS AND EGGS

I'm intentionally not very specific about what type of dairy products to use in these recipes since I think it's perfectly acceptable to choose reduced-fat, skim, whole (full-fat), or lactose-reduced products according to your own dietary needs. Do bear in mind that choosing skim milk over whole milk will yield a slightly less rich finished dish.

All eggs used in this book are large. If you are cholesterol-conscious, you can try substituting Egg Beaters™, or similar egg-replacement products where beaten eggs are called for, or substitute 2 egg whites for 1 whole egg.

FRUITS AND VEGETABLES

Unless otherwise specified, assume that any fruit or vegetable called for is fresh, not canned or frozen.

Some processed fruits and vegetables can be used interchangeably with fresh and some cannot. Frozen cranberries and peaches can be used in cooked or baked dishes instead of fresh. Measure when frozen; if the recipe specifies thawed, thaw before adding to the recipe. I don't find canned fruits to be suitable substitutions for fresh because they are presweetened. For dishes such as salads, where the fruits are used raw, fresh is always best.

I always use fresh lemon or lime juice because I find that the bottled or frozen juice tastes too artificial. Buy a few lemons or limes, squeeze them, then freeze the juice in 1-tablespoon blocks in an ice cube tray. Once frozen, you can empty the tray into a plastic bag. That way you can always have "fresh" lemon juice on hand. Frozen or refrigerated orange juice is acceptable for any recipe calling for orange juice.

Frozen vegetables can also be substituted for fresh, although it's hard to maintain an al dente (tender-crisp) texture once a vegetable has been frozen. As with fruit, measure the vegetables while frozen, then thaw before cooking, unless otherwise specified. Canned vegetables (with the exception of beans and corn) change too much in flavor and consistency to be suitable substitutions for fresh vegetables.

HERBS

When a recipe calls for a chopped herb (such as parsley), it means fresh herbs, unless otherwise specified. If you don't have any fresh herbs on hand, the general rule of thumb is to substitute 1/4 to 1/3 as much dried herbs for the fresh. For example, 3 tablespoons chopped fresh parsley = 2 teaspoons to 1 tablespoon dried parsley.

OILS

Oils add flavor and seriously improve the texture of many dishes. They range from almost flavorless (vegetable oil) to extremely flavorful (chili oil). Not all dishes need highly flavorful oil and in those cases, any vegetable oil that you prefer is the right choice. Oil does go rancid, so it's best stored in the refrigerator if you do not use it too frequently. You can tell if your oil has turned by smelling it; any oil that smells like turpentine should be discarded.

SALT

Salt reacts with certain foods, specifically whole grains and beans, both of which should always be cooked in unsalted liquids. Salt toughens the skin and impedes the absorption of liquids. Beans cooked in salted (or acidic) liquid will not soften properly. Whole grains cooked in salted liquid require a longer cooking time and will not absorb the normal amount of liquid. I recommend adding salt to foods after they are cooked because the flavor is absorbed better. You may not need as much salt since the cooked foods retain more of the saltiness when added after cooking.

SOY PRODUCTS

Soy products are a great asset in any diet, but especially for the vegetarian. They are excellent sources of protein as well as phytoestrogens, isoflavins, and omega-3 fatty acids. The high nutritional profile applies to most soy products, though not to soy sauce or tamari.

DRIED SOYBEANS tend to require long cooking times (about 3 hours) and are not available in cans.

FRESH SOYBEANS are available (usually frozen) in their shells or shelled under the name of edamame. These beans only require a short cooking time. They have a sweet flavor; and are a bright green like lima beans or peas. They make great additions to salads, soups, or stews.

BEAN CURD (TOFU) See page 125.

MISO is fermented soybean paste, sometimes combined with grains such as barley or rice. This paste has a strong flavor that is somewhat bitter and salty.

SEITAN See page 125.

SOY FLOUR is made from ground, heat-treated soybeans. This flour can be used in baked goods to add protein to the final product.

SOYMILK is a liquid extracted from soaked soybeans. Many commercial soybean milk products contain added oil, sugar, and other ingredients. Check the labels.

SOY NUTS Roasted soy nuts are crunchy and are frequently used in trail mix or other snack foods.

SOY SAUCE and TAMARI Soy sauce is a flavoring agent used throughout Asia. Chinese soy sauce (such as La Choy™) tends to be darker and saltier than Japanese soy sauce (such as Kikkoman™). There are also darker and sweeter soy sauces available in Asian markets. Unless otherwise specified, the recipes in this book were prepared using Japanese soy sauce. Real tamari is different from soy; it is actually a by-product of miso and is thicker and stronger than ordinary soy sauce. It's not uncommon, however, for tamari sold in this country to be labeled as soy sauce.

SOY SPROUTS Soy sprouts are sprouted soybeans and are practically always used cooked.

TEMPEH See page 125.

TEXTURED VEGETABLE PROTEIN (TVP) See page 125.

VINEGARS

Interchanging one type of vinegar for another will affect the flavor of the recipe you are preparing. Because some vinegars are more tart than others, the proportions of vinegar to oil or sugar will have to be altered when you change vinegar types. The most commonly available vinegars are:

BALSAMIC VINEGAR Balsamic vinegar is made from very sweet grapes and aged in wooden barrels; a good balsamic vinegar is very mellow and slightly sweet.

APPLE CIDER VINEGAR Made from apples, apple cider vinegar is golden in color, and tastes fruitier than distilled white vinegars.

WHITE VINEGAR Clear in color, white vinegar is fermented from grain alcohol and does not have a very specific flavor, but rather just a tanginess.

FLAVORED VINEGAR Flavored vinegar is usually made from a base of white, wine, or balsamic vinegar to which other flavors are then added. Common flavorings are garlic, herbs, or raspberries and other fruits.

RICE VINEGAR Available in the Asian section of supermarkets or in Asian groceries, rice vinegar is clear in color and somewhat sweet.

WINE VINEGAR Wine vinegar is made from wine grapes. This vinegar, like wine, can be either mellow or coarse and sharp. Red wine vinegar is the most common, but white wine, champagne, and sherry vinegars are also widely available.

SHOPPING FOR RECIPE INGREDIENTS

I write my recipes using very specific amounts of ingredients. The recipes here will call for 1 cup chopped onion instead of 1 medium onion, chopped. I believe that this method eliminates the need to guess; how big, exactly, is a medium onion? On the other hand, it does leave the problem of guessing how many whole onions make up 1 cup chopped. The table below will help eliminate that problem.

ITEM	AMOUNT NEEDED	TO EQUAL
Almonds, whole	4 oz.	1 cup chopped
Apple	1 medium (4 oz.)	1 cup chopped or diced
	1 large (5 1/3 oz.)	1 cup shredded
Asparagus	5 medium (3 1/2 oz.)	1 cup cut
Broccoli	2 medium stalks (9 oz.)	1 cup florets
Cabbage	1 wedge (3 oz.)	1 cup chopped
	1 wedge (2 oz.)	1 cup shredded
Carrot	1 large (6 oz.)	1 cup sliced
		1 cup shredded
		1 cup chopped
Cauliflower	1/4 small head (4 oz.)	1 cup florets
Celery	2 medium stalks (4 oz.)	1 cup sliced
	1 large + 1 medium stalk	1 cup chopped
Cucumber	3/4 medium (6 oz.)	1 cup sliced or chopped
Eggplant	1/4 small (3 1/2 oz.)	1 cup cubed
Green beans	1 1/4 cups whole	1 cup cut (1-inch pieces)
Mushrooms, white	4 medium (3 oz.)	1 cup sliced or chopped
Onion	1 medium (4 oz.)	1 cup chopped
	1 large (7 oz.)	1 cup finely chopped
Peach	1 medium (6 oz.)	1 cup sliced
Pear	1 medium (5 oz.)	1 cup sliced
Pecan halves	4 to 4 1/4 oz.	1 cup chopped
Pepper, bell	1 small (4 1/2 oz.)	1 cup chopped or diced
Potato	1 medium (5 1/2 oz.)	1 cup cubed
	1 medium (4 3/4 oz.)	1 cup shredded
Tomato	1 medium (6 oz.)	1 cup diced or chopped
Walnuts, shelled	4 oz.	1 cup chopped
Zucchini	1 small (3 1/2 oz.)	1 cup sliced
	1 medium (4 1/2 oz.)	1 cup shredded

THE WELL-STOCKED PANTRY

Ideally, a well-stocked pantry (refrigerator included) will have everything in it needed to prepare many of these recipes without having to run to the market. You want to have enough ingredients on hand to "throw together" a meal for unexpected company or when you just don't make it to the supermarket.

The majority of ingredients used in these (and almost all) vegetarian recipes are staples, many of them shelf-stable (items that don't require refrigeration, or at least, not until opening). These include:

- ☐ Bread crumbs
- ☐ Broth (see page 14)
- ☐ Canned corn kernels (8- or 11-ounce can)
- ☐ Canned tomatoes
  - Paste (6-ounce can)
  - Sauce (8-ounce can)
  - Whole peeled, chopped, or diced (14 1/2-ounce can)
- ☐ Cornstarch
- ☐ Flour (all-purpose and whole wheat)
- ☐ Grains (barley and brown rice)
- ☐ Honey
- ☐ Legumes (assorted canned beans, dried lentils, and split peas)
- ☐ Mustard (Dijon and spicy brown or yellow)
- ☐ Nuts (walnuts and/or pecans)
- ☐ Oil (vegetable and olive)
- ☐ Raisins (light or dark)
- ☐ Salt
- ☐ Soymilk (especially for vegan cooking)
- ☐ Soy sauce
- ☐ Sugar
- ☐ Tabasco Sauce or other hot pepper sauce
- ☐ Vegetable bouillon, broth, or stock
- ☐ Vinegar (red wine and distilled white and/or cider)
- ☐ Worcestershire sauce, anchovy-free

HERBS AND SPICES

- [ ] Basil, dried
- [ ] Bay leaves, dried
- [ ] Black pepper, ground or whole
- [ ] Chili powder
- [ ] Cinnamon, ground
- [ ] Curry powder
- [ ] Ginger, dried, ground
- [ ] Gingerroot, fresh
- [ ] Oregano, dried
- [ ] Paprika
- [ ] Parsley (curly or flat-leaf), fresh
- [ ] Red pepper, ground
- [ ] Thyme, dried

FRESH PRODUCE

(One or more of each)

- [ ] Apples
- [ ] Bell peppers (green or red)
- [ ] Carrots
- [ ] Celery
- [ ] Garlic
- [ ] Lemons
- [ ] Lettuce (romaine and/or iceberg)
- [ ] Onions (yellow) and/or leeks
- [ ] Oranges
- [ ] Potatoes
- [ ] Scallions (green onions)
- [ ] Tomatoes

FROZEN PRODUCE

- [ ] Corn
- [ ] Orange and/or apple juice concentrate
- [ ] Peas
- [ ] Spinach, chopped

DAIRY PRODUCTS

(Vegans can use soy variations)

- [ ] Butter or margarine
- [ ] Eggs
- [ ] Milk
- [ ] Parmesan cheese (grated or whole)
- [ ] Yogurt (plain)

COOKING FROM SCRATCH—OR NOT

I certainly prefer to cook everything from scratch, given enough time. Time, however, is a rare commodity nowadays. Many of the recipes in this book use ingredients that have longer-than-convenient cooking times. These ingredients include beans and the longer-cooking grains. In some instances, turning to prepared products is a perfectly fine solution; in others it's not.

BEANS

The advantage of cooking with dried beans over canned is that you have a much wider variety of beans from which to choose. In addition to the many available in the supermarket, health food and gourmet stores carry more interesting varieties, such as rattlesnake beans, scarlet runners, appaloosas, Swedish brown beans, and dozens (probably hundreds, possibly thousands) more. You can also order other appealing varieties by mail (see Mail-Order Sources, page 172). Furthermore, dried beans are not presalted, which is not always the case for canned. (For cooking dried beans, see page 171.)

Canned beans, however, can be fine in many cases. The distinct advantage of having beans ready for a last-minute meal can override the advantages of using dried beans. An acceptable canned bean should be tender but not mushy, should not have much (if any) sludge at the bottom of the can, and certainly should not taste tinny.

BROTH

Broth enhances the flavor of many recipes. There's no doubt in my mind that good homemade vegetable broth is superior to any prepared broth or bouillon (see recipe, page 158). However, just because you don't have any on hand doesn't mean you have to skip a recipe that calls for broth. Vegetable broth or bouillon can be purchased in several forms: frozen or jarred stock is available in gourmet stores or by mail order; canned stock or broth can be found in the supermarket; bouillon cubes (from many manufacturers) and powdered stock is sold in packets or jars in supermarkets and health food stores. All of these can be used with excellent results as part of other recipes. Bear in mind that stock, broth, or bouillon that is only okay when tasted alone may be perfectly fine as part of a bean soup or stew or curry. And like beans, you may have to try a few brands until you find one that is acceptable to you. The one I use most often is Knorr®.

In addition to bouillon labeled "vegetable broth," vegetarian broth is available in the kosher section of your supermarket. Look for bottles of chicken and/or beef broth with the word "parve." Although meat flavored, parve means meat-free and dairy-free.

GRAINS

Although some instant grains (such as couscous, Rizcous, instant grits, and instant polenta) cook up quite well, most grains have to be cooked the old-fashioned, more time-consuming way. I find instant rice to be a totally unacceptable substitute for the "real" thing—which, in fact, takes less than half an hour to cook. My strategy for "instant" grains is to cook a large batch of slower-cooking grains and use it for two or three different recipes. A lot of the recipes call for grains that are already cooked. This allows you to use grains that you have prepared in advance and just reheat for that particular dish.

ELEGANT DINNER

HORS D'OEUVRES

- Creamy Mushroom Pâté (page 26) with crackers
- Cheese platter (brie, goat cheese, blue cheese, hard cheese)
- Artichoke and Parmesan Dip (page 21) with crudité

FIRST COURSE

- Polenta with Gorgonzola Cheese Sauce (page 36), or
- Caesar Salad (page 46), or
- Spinach Salad with Strawberries and Nectarines (page 47)

INTERMEZZO

- Lemon or grapefruit sorbet (small serving as palate cleanser)

ENTRÉES

- Tortellini with Wild Mushroom Sauce (page 105), or
- Black Bean–Polenta Pie (page 83), or
- Risotto alla Milanese (page 112), or
- Mushroom Stroganoff (page 115) over rice or noodles

SIDE DISHES

- Asparagus with Walnuts and Browned Butter (page 131), and
- Basil-Stuffed Baked Tomatoes (page 143), or
- Garlic Green Beans (page 136), and
- Pesto Vegetables (page 142)

DESSERT

- Choose a nice, rich dessert, something you know your guests will love. It's also nice to have a fruit plate for anyone either watching their weight or just too stuffed to indulge. My final touch is usually a confection such as chocolate-covered strawberries or truffles.
- Coffee and tea

APPETIZERS

Artichoke and Parmesan Dip 21

Southwest Corn and Black Bean Dip 22

Hummus 23

Baba Ghanoush 24

Creamy Mushroom Pâté 26

Chopped Tomato and Olive Spread 27

Guacamole 28

Dolmas 30

Old-Fashioned Stuffed Mushrooms 32

Mini Vegetable Dumplings with Asian Dipping Sauce 34

Polenta with Gorgonzola Cheese Sauce 36

Greek Cucumber Salad 37

Tempeh Fingers with Honey Mustard Dip 38

IPS

Back in the 1950s—when the perfect host/ess was serving chips and onion dip, pigs in blankets, and those famous cocktail meatballs prepared in a sauce of equal parts grape jelly and ketchup—crudité (at that time known simply as "raw vegetables") consisted of carrot and celery sticks and cucumber slices. That was all, unless you were daring and included a cherry tomato or two. Nowadays, in addition to becoming more creative and health conscious about our dips, we serve them with a variety of interesting vegetables, taking the experience light-years beyond the original concept of chips and dip.

Some of the dippers I like to use (in addition to celery and carrot sticks, cucumber slices, and the occasional cherry tomato) are:

• raw or blanched broccoli or cauliflower florets

• rutabaga sticks

• zucchini sticks

• jicama sticks

• Jerusalem artichoke rounds

• Belgian endive leaves

• radishes (whole red or white), or daikon sticks

• whole button mushrooms

• red, yellow, orange, green, or purple bell pepper slices

• snow peas or snap peas

• kohlrabi sticks

Presentation of the dip can also be more interesting than just a simple bowl. Be creative. Hollow out a small loaf of bread and fill it with dip. Or create bowls out of vegetables. Cut the tops off of bell peppers and discard the seeds, or scoop out the inside of a large tomato. Cooked artichokes or heads of cabbage or cauliflower can be carved to make room for dips.

ARTICHOKE AND PARMESAN DIP

MAKES 3/4 CUP • SERVES 4 TO 6

For a pretty presentation, serve this dip in a hollowed-out cooked artichoke. Guests can dip the outer leaves as well as other assorted crudité.

1/3 cup oil-marinated artichoke hearts, drained
1/4 cup mayonnaise
2 tablespoons sliced scallions (white and green parts)
1 clove garlic, minced
1/4 cup plain yogurt
1/4 cup grated Parmesan cheese
1/4 teaspoon ground black pepper

1 Place the artichoke hearts, mayonnaise, scallions, and garlic in a blender container. Cover and blend mix until smooth.

2 Transfer to a medium bowl and stir in the yogurt, Parmesan cheese, and pepper.

VARIATION Add 2 tablespoons chopped fresh parsley when you stir in the Parmesan cheese.

APPETIZERS

SOUTHWEST CORN AND BLACK BEAN DIP

MAKES 3 CUPS • SERVES 12 TO 20

This recipe makes a large amount of dip, but you can easily halve the recipe. It's best when left to "age" overnight. Serve with tortilla chips, of course! Because this dip is so chunky, it's also a perfect salsa; it's delicious with tacos or similar foods.

1 1/2 cups chopped tomatoes

1/2 cup cooked black beans (cooked from dry; or canned, drained)

1/2 cup cooked fresh corn kernels, or frozen, thawed or canned, drained

1/2 cup chopped onion

1/4 cup chopped canned chiles, drained (optional)

1/4 cup mild enchilada sauce

1 clove garlic, minced

1/2 teaspoon chili powder

1/4 teaspoon ground cumin

1/8 teaspoon salt, or to taste

In a medium bowl, combine all the ingredients. Refrigerate overnight.

VARIATION Add 1/4 cup chopped fresh cilantro.

LO LACTO-OVO L LACTO V VEGAN ✳ VEGAN VARIATION M MAKE-AHEAD

HUMMUS

**MAKES 1 1/2 CUPS • SERVES 3 TO 4 AS A SPREAD OR
6 TO 8 AS A DIP**

This Middle Eastern spread, when not used to fill a sandwich, is usually spread on a small plate, drizzled with olive oil, and garnished with olives, pepperoncini (small pickled Italian peppers), and a splash of hot sauce in the center, then scooped up with fresh pita bread. Yum!

1 1/2 cups cooked chickpeas (cooked from dry; or canned, drained)

3 tablespoons tahini (sesame paste)

3 tablespoons fresh lemon juice

2 tablespoons vegetable oil

1 tablespoon olive oil

2 cloves garlic, minced

1/4 teaspoon ground cumin

1/8 teaspoon salt, or to taste

Place all the ingredients in a food processor container fitted with a steel blade. Cover and process blend until pureed.

VARIATION Add 1/4 cup chopped scallions (green parts only) and Tabasco™ hot sauce to taste.

BABA GHANOUSH

MAKES 1 1/4 CUPS • SERVES 4 TO 6 AS A SPREAD OR 3 TO 4 AS A SANDWICH FILLING

In the Middle East you're likely to find this in pita bread sandwiches; here, it's usually served as a dip, with pita bread on the side. This version is fairly smooth; the chopped variation below is a bit more traditional.

1 medium eggplant (about 1 pound)
1/4 cup lightly packed fresh parsley leaves
3 tablespoons fresh lemon juice
3 tablespoons tahini (sesame paste)
2 cloves garlic, minced

1 Prick the whole eggplant in several places with a fork. Place on a grill or under a broiler. Cook, turning about every 5 minutes, until charred all over (about 20 minutes total).

2 Cut the eggplant in half, scoop out the flesh, and discard the skin. Let cool.

3 Place the eggplant, parsley, lemon juice, tahini, and garlic in the container of a food processor fitted with a steel blade. Pulse until the parsley is finely chopped. Let stand at least one hour to let the flavors meld.

VARIATION Instead of using a food processor, finely chop the eggplant by hand, then stir in the remaining ingredients.

CREAMY MUSHROOM PÂTÉ

MAKES 1 2/3 CUPS • SERVES 6 TO 8

Because the delicate flavor of this spread is easily lost, I like to serve it with bread rather than crackers. You can certainly make this spread ahead of time—just refrigerate it until one hour before serving, then let it stand at room temperature so it is softened to spreading consistency.

2 tablespoons butter or margarine

3 tablespoons minced shallots

2 cups finely chopped wild mushrooms (shiitake, porcini, Portobello)

1/2 cup chopped fresh parsley

1/4 teaspoon dried savory or thyme

One 8-ounce package cream cheese, cut into 8 cubes

3 tablespoons heavy cream

1 Melt the butter or margarine in a medium skillet over medium-high heat.

2 Add the shallots; cook, stirring, until softened, about 1 minute. Add the mushrooms; cook, stirring until softened, about 5 minutes. Continue cooking until any mushroom liquid has evaporated. Stir in the parsley and savory; cook, stirring, 30 seconds.

3 Remove from heat. Stir in the cream cheese, 1 ounce at a time, until melted and completely combined. Stir in heavy cream. Chill.

VARIATION Mushroom Tartlets: Spoon a rounded teaspoonful of the spread into baked 1-inch tartlet shells. Makes about 40.

LO LACTO-OVO L LACTO V VEGAN ✳ VEGAN VARIATION M MAKE-AHEAD

CHOPPED TOMATO AND OLIVE SPREAD

MAKES 1 CUP • SERVES 4 TO 6

The consistency here is somewhere between a salsa and a spread; you really need to spoon it on bread or crackers rather than spread it. Although you can use ordinary canned black olives in this recipe, I prefer to make the extra effort (and expense) to find imported olives like kalamata, since the spread really gets its character from the type of olive that you choose.

1 cup finely diced tomato
1/4 cup chopped pitted black olives
2 cloves garlic, minced
1 teaspoon fresh lemon juice
1 teaspoon olive oil
1/8 teaspoon salt

In a medium bowl, stir together all the ingredients. Let stand at least one hour to let the flavors meld.

VARIATION Add 1 tablespoon chopped fresh parsley or basil.

GUACAMOLE

MAKES 1 CUP • SERVES 2 TO 4

This is a very basic recipe. I usually prepare it with all the variations when serving it as a dip. When using it as an ingredient for other Mexican dishes such as Burritos (page 85), I use the plain recipe below. People like to eat lots of guacamole, so you may want to double the recipe. I prefer to use Hass avocados (the ones with the rough skin), but if they aren't available any ripe avocado will do—ripeness is very important to a good guacamole. To check ripeness, gently press the avocado with your thumb. If it feels like a rock, it is not ripe; if it gives a little, it probably is ripe; if it gives a lot, it's probably overripe.

1 cup avocado pulp (1 small to medium avocado)
2 tablespoons fresh lime juice
2 tablespoons chopped scallions (white and green parts)
1 tablespoon sour cream
2 cloves garlic, minced
1/2 fresh or pickled jalapeño, seeded and minced

In a medium bowl, mash the avocado with a fork until smooth or slightly chunky (as you prefer). Add the remaining ingredients and mix.

VARIATION Add 1/2 cup seeded chopped tomatoes and/or 2 to 4 tablespoons chopped fresh cilantro.

VEGAN VARIATION Omit the sour cream.

100 BEST VEGETARIAN RECIPES

DOLMAS (STUFFED GRAPE LEAVES)

MAKES 16 TO 18 DOLMAS • SERVES 4 TO 6

These are very traditional Greek *dolmas*. You can use either grape or vine leaves, but I find that grape leaves are milder and more pleasant tasting. They can be served warm or cold. For a different filling, omit the sun-dried tomatoes and dill. Add 2 tablespoons finely chopped dried apricots, 1 tablespoon of dried currants, and 1 tablespoon chopped fresh mint when you add the parsley.

One 16-ounce jar grape leaves
1 teaspoon olive oil
1/4 cup chopped onion
1/4 cup chopped celery
1 clove garlic, minced
2 cups vegetable broth (homemade, page 158, or store-bought), divided
1/4 cup white rice
3 tablespoons finely chopped, drained oil-marinated sun-dried tomatoes
1/4 cup chopped fresh parsley
2 tablespoons snipped fresh dill
1 cup water
1 tablespoon fresh lemon juice

1 Drain the grape leaves and place in a large bowl. Cover with fresh water and let stand 5 minutes. Drain.

2 In a 1-quart saucepan, heat the oil over medium-high heat. Add the onion, celery, and garlic; cook, stirring, until softened, about 2 minutes. Add 1/2 cup of the broth; bring to a boil. Add the rice, reduce heat, and simmer, covered, 20 minutes or until liquid is absorbed. Stir in the sun-dried tomatoes, parsley, and dill.

3 Trim the stem from a grape leaf. Lay the leaf flat on the counter. Place 1 level tablespoon of the filling near the stem end of the leaf. Fold the sides of the leaf over the filling and then roll the leaf away from you, forming a small log. Repeat until all the filling has been used.

4 Place half of the remaining leaves in the bottom of a 3-quart saucepan. Place the grape-leaf logs in the bottom of the skillet, seam side down. Top with remaining grape leaves.

5 Pour the remaining 1 1/2 cups of broth and the water and lemon juice into the saucepan, adding extra water, if necessary, to cover the stuffed grape leaves. Place a plate over the leaves to prevent the logs from rising to the surface while cooking. Bring to a boil. Reduce heat and simmer, 45 minutes, uncovered. Remove from saucepan and let cool.

VARIATION Place 1/4 cup pine nuts (*pignoli*) into a dry skillet. Cook over medium-low heat, stirring, until slightly browned, about 2 minutes. Let cool and add when you add the herbs in step 2.

OLD-FASHIONED STUFFED MUSHROOMS

MAKES 16 MUSHROOMS • SERVES 3 TO 4

This was the only way to stuff mushrooms when I was a kid. Back then, the adventurous cook might use flavored bread crumbs instead of plain. For a slightly zestier version, add 1/4 cup grated Parmesan cheese and 1 more minced clove of garlic.

16 medium white mushrooms (about 14 ounces)
1 tablespoon butter, margarine, or vegetable oil
1/4 cup minced onion
1 small clove garlic, minced
1/3 cup dry bread crumbs (plain or flavored)
2 tablespoons chopped fresh parsley
1/4 teaspoon salt, or to taste
1/8 teaspoon ground black pepper

1 Preheat oven to 375°F.

2 Wipe the mushrooms clean with a damp cloth and separate the caps from the stems. Set the caps aside and chop the stems.

3 In a medium skillet, melt the butter or margarine (or heat the oil) over medium-high heat. Add the onion and garlic; cook, stirring, until softened, 1 to 2 minutes. Add the chopped mushroom stems; cook, stirring, until softened, about 3 minutes. If mushrooms give off liquid, cook until it evaporates. Remove from heat. Stir in bread crumbs, parsley, salt, and pepper.

4 Spoon about 1 tablespoon of filling into each of the mushroom caps, place into a 9 x 13-inch baking pan. Bake 12 minutes or until heated through.

VARIATION Herb-Stuffed Mushrooms: Use seasoned bread crumbs plus 1/2 teaspoon chopped fresh basil and 1/8 teaspoon chopped fresh thyme.

STUFFED MUSHROOMS

Stuffed mushrooms have been a favorite party dish as far back as I can remember. If you're planning to serve them as finger foods, use small or button mushrooms that guests can pop into their mouths in a single bite. Medium or large stuffed mushrooms are more appropriate as appetizers, eaten on a plate with a fork and knife. The recipe here calls for medium mushrooms, but you can use smaller ones; just go by the given weight, ignore the number called for, and use less filling per mushroom.

MINI VEGETABLE DUMPLINGS WITH ASIAN DIPPING SAUCE

MAKES 24 TO 28 DUMPLINGS • SERVES 4 TO 6

If you cannot find round dumpling skins, buy wonton wrappers and cut them into rounds using a 3- to 3 1/2-inch cookie or biscuit cutter. You can prepare the dipping sauce and fill the dumplings in advance, but cook the dumplings just before serving.

ASIAN DIPPING SAUCE
3 tablespoons water

2 tablespoons soy sauce

2 teaspoons mirin (rice wine) or dry sherry

1 teaspoon thinly sliced scallion

1 teaspoon minced fresh gingerroot

1 teaspoon sugar

1 clove garlic, minced

DUMPLINGS
1 tablespoon vegetable oil

1 1/2 teaspoons minced fresh gingerroot

2 cloves garlic, minced

1 1/2 cups fresh mung bean sprouts

1 cup lightly packed chopped spinach

1/2 cup chopped mushrooms

1/2 cup coarsely shredded carrots

1/4 cup chopped scallions (white and green parts)

1 teaspoon soy sauce

1/2 teaspoon sesame oil

24 to 28 dumpling wrappers or 15 wonton wrappers

1 For the sauce, in a small bowl, stir together the water, soy sauce, mirin or sherry, scallion, gingerroot, sugar, and garlic. Set aside.

2 For the dumplings, in a medium skillet, heat the vegetable oil over high heat. Add the gingerroot and garlic; cook, stirring, 10 seconds. Add the bean sprouts, spinach, mushrooms, carrots, and scallions. Cook, stirring, until vegetables are tender and any liquid has evaporated, about 5 minutes. Stir in the soy sauce and sesame oil. Let stand until cool enough to handle.

LO LACTO-OVO   **L** LACTO   **V** VEGAN   **✳** VEGAN VARIATION   **M** MAKE-AHEAD

3 Place 1 rounded teaspoon of the spinach filling in the center of a dumpling wrapper. Wet the edges with water. Fold in half to form half-moons and pleat the edges in an accordion pleat; press the edges together to seal. Repeat with remaining wrappers and filling.

4 Drop the sealed dumplings into salted boiling water and cook until the dumplings rise to the surface and look translucent, 1 to 2 minutes.

VARIATION Add 1/4 cup chopped water chestnuts to the filling for a crunchier texture.

POLENTA WITH GORGONZOLA CHEESE SAUCE

MAKES 4 MOLDED POLENTA AND 1 CUP SAUCE • SERVES 4

This is a very creamy polenta, like a dense pudding. You can prepare the polenta in advance, pour it into cups, then chill until you want to serve them. To reheat, place in the microwave or in a water bath in the oven. They unmold with good result. You can skip the Gorgonzola sauce and use any warmed pasta sauce instead.

POLENTA
2 cups milk
1 3/4 cups water
2 tablespoons butter or margarine
1/2 teaspoon salt, or to taste
1/2 cup yellow cornmeal (polenta)

SAUCE
1 tablespoon butter or margarine
1 tablespoon all-purpose flour
1/4 teaspoon paprika
1/2 cup vegetable broth (homemade, page 158, or
  store-bought)
1/4 cup half-and-half
1/4 cup packed soft Gorgonzola or other creamy blue cheese
2 tablespoons grated Parmesan cheese
1/8 teaspoon ground red pepper

1 Grease four 6-ounce custard cups.

2 For the polenta, in a 2-quart saucepan over medium-high heat, bring milk, water, 2 tablespoons of the butter or margarine, and the salt to a boil, stirring frequently.

3 With the liquid still boiling, sprinkle the cornmeal 1 tablespoon at a time over the liquid, stirring constantly so that no lumps form. Reduce heat and simmer 35 to 45 minutes, stirring very frequently, until the polenta remains mounded when dropped from a spoon. Divide polenta evenly among custard cups; let stand 10 minutes.

4 For the sauce, in a 1-quart saucepan, melt the 1 tablespoon butter or margarine over medium-high heat. Add the flour and paprika; stir until absorbed. Stir in the broth and half-and-half. Cook, stirring, until mixture comes to a boil. Add both cheeses and pepper and stir until cheeses are melted.

5 Place 2 tablespoons of sauce on each of 4 small serving plates, unmold the polenta onto plates, and top each with some of the remaining sauce.

VARIATION Use a different sauce, such as Fresh Tomato Sauce (page 161).

L
M

GREEK CUCUMBER SALAD

MAKES 1 CUP • SERVES 4 TO 6

I tasted a wonderful cucumber spread at a Greek restaurant and tried to duplicate it right after, while the flavor was still fresh in my mind. This is especially tasty served with baked pita wedges: brush with oil (or oil mixed with crushed garlic and/or 1/8 teaspoon dried oregano) and bake at 350°F 10 to 15 minutes or until crisp.

1/2 cup crumbled feta cheese
4 ounces cream cheese, softened (4 ounces)
1/3 cup sour cream
1/2 cup finely chopped, seeded cucumber
1 tablespoon thinly sliced scallions (green parts only)
1/8 teaspoon ground black pepper

1 Place the feta, cream cheese, and sour cream into a blender or a food processor container fitted with a metal blade. Process until smooth.

2 Spoon into a medium bowl. Stir in cucumber, scallions, and pepper.

VARIATION Add 1/4 cup chopped radish when you add the cucumber. For a lower-fat version, substitute fat-free sour cream or yogurt for the sour cream.

APPETIZERS

TEMPEH FINGERS WITH HONEY MUSTARD DIP

MAKES 22 TEMPEH FINGERS • SERVES 6 TO 8

Tempeh is made from fermented cooked soybeans that are then formed into blocks. The texture of Tempeh Fingers is similar to French fries.

HONEY MUSTARD DIP
1/2 cup plain yogurt

3 tablespoons mayonnaise

3 tablespoons honey mustard

TEMPEH FINGERS
Oil for deep-frying

One 8-ounce package tempeh, sliced into 1/4-inch "fingers"

1 For the dip, in a small bowl, stir together the yogurt, mayonnaise, and honey mustard; set aside.

2 For the Tempeh Fingers, pour 1/4 inch oil into a large skillet. Heat the oil until it bubbles when a small piece of tempeh is dropped in. Working with 4 to 6 fingers at a time, cook, over medium-high heat, until golden on bottom; turn and cook second side. Drain on paper towels. Serve with Honey Mustard Dip.

VARIATION Tempeh Croutons: Cut tempeh into 1/2-inch cubes and cook as for Fingers. Serve over salads.

VEGAN VARIATION Use warm marinara sauce as the dipping sauce for the Tempeh Fingers instead of the honey mustard dip.

100 BEST VEGETARIAN RECIPES

LO LACTO-OVO **L** LACTO **V** VEGAN **✴** VEGAN VARIATION **M** MAKE-AHEAD

SALADS

The Gelles Family Salad 40

Tomato and Feta Cheese Salad 42

Cucumber Fennel Salad 43

Israeli Salad 43

Coleslaw 44

Caesar Salad 46

Spinach Salad with Strawberries and Nectarines 47

Tabbouleh 48

Potato Salad 50

Marinated Chickpea Salad 52

Quinoa Salad 54

Shredded Carrot and Jicama Salad 56

THE GELLES FAMILY SALAD

MAKES 7 CUPS • SERVES 4

My mother's idea of a perfect salad is a wedge of iceburg lettuce with lots of Russian dressing, but Dad always preferred romaine, so romaine was the primary salad in our family. Dad's the dressing maker; his formula is once around the bowl with oil and twice with vinegar. So here's our salad: you can add as many additional ingredients as you like, but if you add a lot you may want to increase the dressing. I sometimes add a touch of garlic powder to the dressing.

8 cups bite-size pieces romaine lettuce
2 tablespoons red wine vinegar
1 tablespoon vegetable oil
Pinch salt
Pinch freshly ground black pepper
*Add ons: Olives, croutons, carrots, tomato, cucumber, sliced onion, bell peppers, grated, shredded, or crumbled cheese, cooked beans, apples, nuts, herbs

Place the lettuce in a large salad bowl. Add the vinegar, oil, salt, and pepper. Toss until combined.

LO LACTO-OVO **L** LACTO **V** VEGAN ✷ VEGAN VARIATION **M** MAKE-AHEAD

SALADS

I think many people consider the word "lettuce" to be synonymous with the word "salad." Although in the past a mixture of lettuce and tomato was the most commonly available salad, nowadays anything goes. Pasta salad, rice salad, potato salad, bean salad, and even bread salad add interest and zing to meals.

Furthermore, lettuce is not just iceberg anymore. Look for exciting lettuces and greens, such as mâche, oak leaf (red or green), arugula, and endive, not to mention spinach, leaf (red or green), chicory, romaine, and Boston (or butter). There are no hard and fast rules—except that the end result taste delicious.

TOMATO AND FETA CHEESE SALAD
MAKES 3 1/2 CUPS • SERVES 4 TO 6

Kalamata olives are really excellent in this salad. If you can find them already pitted, you will save yourself a lot of work. You can also add diced mozzarella cheese instead of the feta cheese, or add extra feta and serve this as a main course salad for 2 or 3.

3 cups diced tomatoes
1/2 cup halved pitted black olives
1/3 cup sliced red onion
1 tablespoon extra virgin olive oil
1 tablespoon red wine vinegar
1/2 cup crumbled feta cheese
Freshly ground black pepper, to taste

In a large bowl, toss together the tomatoes, olives, and onion. Add the oil and vinegar. Toss to combine. Add the feta cheese, grind the pepper over the top, and toss again.

VARIATION Add 1/2 teaspoon dried oregano with the oil and vinegar.

VEGAN VARIATION Substitute sliced hearts of palm for the feta cheese.

CUCUMBER FENNEL SALAD

MAKES 3 CUPS • SERVES 4

The flavors of the fennel and basil are somewhat similar and complement each other. If you are not fond of the taste of licorice, substitute celery for the fennel and parsley or dill for the basil.

2 cups sliced cucumbers
1 cup sliced fennel
2 tablespoons chopped fresh basil
1 tablespoon extra virgin olive oil
1 tablespoon white wine vinegar

In a large bowl, combine the cucumbers, fennel, and basil. Add the oil and vinegar and toss to combine.

ISRAELI SALAD

MAKES 3 CUPS • SERVES 4 TO 6

It's common practice in Israel to have salad for breakfast. A bowl of fantastic vegetables is placed on the table, then everyone dices up their own salad. The vegetables I've suggested here are just a few of the many possibilities. Radishes and even pickles are also popular ingredients in these salads.

1 1/2 cups diced tomatoes
1 cup diced cucumbers
1/2 cup diced green bell pepper
2 tablespoons chopped onion
2 teaspoons extra virgin olive oil
1/4 teaspoon salt, or to taste
Freshly ground black pepper, to taste

In a medium bowl, combine all the ingredients.

VARIATION If you prefer tart salads, you can add red wine vinegar or white wine vinegar, to taste.

SALADS

COLESLAW

MAKES 4 1/2 CUPS • SERVES 6 TO 8

You can serve this right away, but it's really better if you let it stand at least one hour to let the cabbage soften. Substitute red cabbage for some of the green cabbage for a more festive presentation.

5 cups shredded red and green cabbage
1 cup shredded carrots
1/2 cup mayonnaise
2 tablespoons plain yogurt
2 teaspoons white vinegar
1/2 teaspoon salt, or to taste
Freshly ground black pepper, to taste

1 In a large bowl, toss together the cabbage and carrots.

2 In a small bowl, stir together the remaining ingredients. Pour the dressing over the salad and let stand at least 30 minutes for flavors to meld.

VARIATION Stir in 1/4 to 1/2 teaspoon celery seed.

VEGAN VARIATION Add sliced cucumber, celery, and/or onion to the cabbage and use the following dressing: 1/3 cup vegetable oil, 1/4 cup white vinegar, 1 1/2 teaspoons sugar, 2 cloves garlic, minced, and salt and black pepper to taste.

CAESAR SALAD

MAKES 7 CUPS • SERVES 4 TO 6

Who needs anchovies for an outstanding Caesar salad? Not me!
For a creamier dressing, prepare it in a blender or food processor.
You can wash and tear the lettuce and prepare the dressing in
advance, but don't toss until serving time.

1 egg
1 tablespoon extra virgin olive oil
1 tablespoon minced oil-marinated sun-dried tomatoes
1 clove garlic, crushed in a press
1 1/2 tablespoons fresh lemon juice
1 teaspoon red wine vinegar
1 teaspoon Dijon mustard
1/4 teaspoon anchovy-free Worcestershire sauce
1/4 teaspoon salt, or to taste
8 cups bite-size pieces romaine lettuce
Freshly ground black pepper, to taste
3 tablespoons grated Parmesan cheese
Croutons (homemade or store-bought)

1 Place the egg in boiling water for 1 minute. Crack the egg
and separate, discarding the white. Place the yolk in a large
salad bowl. Add the oil, sun-dried tomatoes, and garlic. Using
a whisk, stir until combined. Add the lemon juice, vinegar,
mustard, Worcestershire sauce, and salt. Whisk until
completely combined.

2 Add the lettuce to the bowl. Toss until the dressing coats
the lettuce. Grind some pepper over the salad and sprinkle
with Parmesan and croutons. Toss again and serve.

VARIATION Add tomatoes, cucumbers, or other vegetables
to the salad.

VEGAN VARIATION Omit egg yolk and Parmesan cheese.

SPINACH SALAD WITH STRAWBERRIES AND NECTARINES

MAKES 6 CUPS • SERVES 4 TO 6

This is a really special salad. I prefer to use baby spinach, but torn regular spinach is fine, too. As always with spinach, be sure to rinse it very thoroughly to make sure you've gotten rid of any hidden sand or grit. For a more traditional spinach salad, omit the fruit and sunflower seeds and substitute 2 cups sliced mushrooms and 1/3 cup thinly sliced red onion.

6 cups lightly packed, bite-size pieces fresh spinach

1 cup pitted and sliced nectarines

1 cup hulled and sliced strawberries

1 tablespoon vegetable oil

1 tablespoon fresh lemon juice

1 tablespoon balsamic vinegar

1 teaspoon sugar

1 teaspoon dry mustard

1 tablespoon sunflower seeds (optional)

1 In a large bowl, toss together the spinach, nectarines, and strawberries.

2 In a small bowl, stir together the oil, lemon juice, vinegar, sugar, and dry mustard. Pour the dressing over the salad and toss to combine. Sprinkle with sunflower seeds and serve.

VARIATION Substitute peaches for the nectarines and raspberries for the strawberries.

SALADS

TABBOULEH

MAKES 3 1/3 CUPS • SERVES 4 TO 6

The key elements in this Middle Eastern salad are bulgur, chopped vegetables, and mint. The dressing is quite light and the mint adds refreshing flavor. If you are using bulgur that is already cooked, use 1 1/2 cups cooked bulgur and omit step 1.

1 cup water
1/2 cup bulgur
3/4 cup chopped tomato
3/4 cup chopped cucumber
1/3 cup chopped fresh parsley
1/4 cup chopped fresh mint
1/4 cup chopped scallions
1 1/2 tablespoons olive oil
1 tablespoon fresh lemon juice
1 teaspoon red wine vinegar
1/4 teaspoon salt, or to taste
1/8 teaspoon ground black pepper

1 In a 1-quart saucepan, bring the water to a boil. Add the bulgur and return to a boil. Reduce heat and simmer, covered, 20 minutes or until the liquid is absorbed. Let cool.

2 In a large bowl, toss the bulgur, tomatoes, cucumber, parsley, mint, and scallions until combined.

3 In a small bowl, stir together the oil, lemon juice, vinegar, salt, and pepper. Pour over the salad and toss to combine.

VARIATION Substitute 1/4 cup extra parsley if you do not have mint on hand or are not fond of it.

POTATO SALAD

MAKES 3 CUPS • SERVES 4 TO 6

I like to use boiling potatoes for potato salad because I prefer their texture to baking potatoes. You can jazz up potato salad by adding shredded carrots, chopped celery, cooked peas, or chopped fresh parsley or dill. Or stir curry powder into the dressing for a curried potato salad.

3 cups sliced, cooked potatoes (peeled or unpeeled)
1/4 cup mayonnaise
2 tablespoons plain yogurt
1 teaspoon apple cider vinegar
1 teaspoon grated onion or onion juice
1/2 teaspoon spicy brown mustard
1/4 teaspoon salt, or to taste
Freshly ground black pepper, to taste

Place the potatoes in a large bowl. In a small bowl, stir together the mayonnaise, yogurt, vinegar, onion, mustard, and salt. Pour the dressing over the potatoes, grind pepper on top, and toss to combine.

VARIATION Add 1/2 cup finely chopped green pepper and/or celery.

VEGAN VARIATION Substitute the following dressing: In a blender combine 1/2 cup chopped parsley, 2 tablespoons extra virgin olive oil, and 1 tablespoon red wine vinegar. Cover and blend until finely chopped. Pour over potatoes, stir in 1/3 cup thinly sliced scallions, and add salt and black pepper to taste.

MARINATED CHICKPEA SALAD

MAKES 2 1/2 CUPS • SERVES 4

You can use any cooked legume for this salad. You can also omit the olives and/or add diced roasted red peppers. For more color, add the red and/or green pepper as suggested in the variation, or add thinly sliced scallions and/or chopped parsley.

1 1/2 cups cooked chickpeas (cooked from dry; or canned, drained)

1/2 cup finely chopped celery

1/2 cup chopped black olives

1/4 cup finely chopped onion

3 tablespoons white vinegar

2 tablespoons extra virgin olive oil

1 teaspoon dried oregano

1 clove garlic, minced

1/8 teaspoon salt, or to taste

Freshly ground black pepper, to taste

Place all the ingredients in a large bowl and toss to combine. Let stand at least 30 minutes before serving.

VARIATION Add 1/3 cup each finely chopped red and/or green bell pepper.

LO LACTO-OVO **L** LACTO **V** VEGAN ✳ VEGAN VARIATION **M** MAKE-AHEAD

100 BEST VEGETARIAN RECIPES

QUINOA SALAD

MAKES 4 CUPS • SERVES 6 TO 8

Stirring in extra olive oil at the end of the cooking time really boosts the flavor. Add sautéed peppers and fresh basil for Mediterranean flare.

1 cup quinoa (white or red)
2 teaspoons olive oil
1 cup shiitake mushrooms, quartered
1/2 cup chopped onion
1 cup vegetable broth (homemade, page 158, or store-bought)
1 cup water
1/2 teaspoon dried oregano
1/2 cup green bean pieces
1/8 teaspoon salt, or to taste
1/8 teaspoon ground black pepper
2 tablespoons olive oil
2 tablespoons lemon juice
2 teaspoons wine vinegar

1 Place the quinoa in a large bowl; fill bowl with cool water, then drain. Repeat 4 more times or until the water no longer looks soapy.

2 In a 2-quart saucepan, heat the oil over medium-high heat. Add the mushrooms and onion; cook, stirring, until mushrooms are cooked, about 4 minutes.

3 Add the broth and the water; bring to a boil. Stir in the quinoa and oregano; return to a boil. Reduce heat and simmer, covered, for 15 minutes. Add green beans, cover, and cook 5 minutes longer.

4 Remove from heat; stir in the salt, and pepper. Let cool.

5 Add the oil, lemon juice, and vinegar. Toss.

VARIATION Add 3 tablespoons chopped fresh basil when you stir in the salt.

LO LACTO-OVO **L** LACTO **V** VEGAN **✳** VEGAN VARIATION **M** MAKE-AHEAD

SHREDDED CARROT AND JICAMA SALAD

MAKES 3 CUPS • SERVES 4 TO 6

This is a very lightly dressed salad. If you're comfortable with a more conventional dressing, just add extra oil. The coriander flavor is very subtle here—add more to taste, if you like.

2 cups coarsely shredded carrots
1 1/2 cups peeled, coarsely shredded jicama
1 tablespoon apple cider vinegar
2 teaspoons vegetable oil
1/8 teaspoon ground coriander
1/8 teaspoon salt, or to taste

In a medium bowl, toss together the carrots and jicama. Add the remaining ingredients and toss to combine.

VARIATION Stir in 1/2 cup finely diced fresh pineapple or drained, crushed, canned pineapple.

LO LACTO-OVO L LACTO V VEGAN ✳ VEGAN VARIATION M MAKE-AHEAD

100 BEST VEGETARIAN RECIPES

SOUPS

SPRING VEGETABLE SOUP

MAKES 4 CUPS • SERVES 4 TO 6

This very light, broth-based soup is just perfect for a simple meal, even brunch. You can use frozen peas if you can't find fresh ones.

4 cups vegetable broth (homemade, page 158,
  or store-bought)
1/2 cup julienned carrot
1/2 cup thinly sliced white mushrooms
1/4 cup fresh shelled peas
4 to 6 thin asparagus, quartered lengthwise and cut into
  2-inch pieces
6 snow peas, julienned
2 tablespoons chopped fresh parsley

1 In a 2-quart saucepan, bring the broth to a boil over medium-high heat. Add the carrot, mushrooms, and shelled peas; simmer, uncovered, 3 minutes or until carrots and peas are tender.

2 Add the asparagus, snow peas, and parsley; simmer 2 minutes longer.

VARIATION Use almost any julienned seasonal vegetable.

EGETABLE BROTH

I don't usually think of broth as my favorite soup, but broth is probably the most important soup base in this book (Mighty Vegetable Broth, page 158). It is a perfect low-calorie snack, and the base of many interesting recipes. It's broth that makes risotto breathtaking, pilafs exciting, stews fascinating, and other soups scintillating. The fact is, broth frequently makes the difference between watery, "thin" dishes and interesting, complex flavors.

It's my practice to make batches of broth whenever I have leftover vegetables. Freeze the broth in 1-cup portions, then just defrost as many packages as cups of broth are needed.

If you don't have any broth on hand, there are many commercial vegetable broths available. See page 14 for more on this subject.

BUTTERMILK BROCCOLI SOUP

MAKES 5 1/2 CUPS • SERVES 6 TO 8

This soup is equally delicious warm or chilled. You can always substitute other vegetables, so if you don't have broccoli on hand, but do have zucchini, this could become Buttermilk Zucchini Soup or almost anything else you can think of.

1 1/2 teaspoons vegetable oil

1 cup sliced leeks (white and light green parts only)

2 cups vegetable broth (homemade, page 158, or store-bought)

2 cups water

4 cups broccoli florets

1/3 cup chopped fresh dill

1/4 cup white rice

2 cups buttermilk

1/8 teaspoon ground red pepper

1 In a 3-quart saucepan, heat the oil over medium-high heat. Add the leeks; cook, stirring, until softened, about 1 minute.

2 Add the broth and water; bring to a boil. Add the broccoli, dill, and rice; return to a boil. Reduce heat and simmer, uncovered, 30 minutes.

3 Place the soup in a blender or food processor. Cover and puree. (You may have to do this in more than one batch.)

4 Return to pot and stir in buttermilk and red pepper. Reheat if necessary.

VARIATION For a chilled version, don't reheat after stirring in the buttermilk; cool in refrigerator instead. Serve with dollops of plain yogurt.

FOUR-IN-ONE TOMATO SOUP

MAKES 5 1/2 CUPS • SERVES 6 TO 8

Soup #1: Cooked as originally written, it's an unusual, delicious Curried Tomato Soup, perfect to impress company.

Soup #2: Omit the spices and you have a lovely basic tomato soup.

Soup #3: Make soup #2, stir in 1/4 cup heavy cream and a pinch of nutmeg, and you have a dynamite Creamy Tomato Soup.

Soup #4: Curried Spinach and Tomato Soup: Add a 10-ounce package frozen chopped spinach after you've pureed the Curried Tomato Soup. Return to heat and cook until spinach is heated through.

1 tablespoon vegetable oil

1 cup chopped onion

1 cup peeled, chopped tart apples

1 tablespoon curry powder

1 teaspoon ground coriander

1/2 teaspoon ground ginger

1/2 teaspoon ground cardamom

1/2 teaspoon ground turmeric

One 28-ounce can crushed tomatoes

2 cups vegetable broth (homemade, page 158, or store-bought)

1 cup water

3 tablespoons firmly packed light or dark brown sugar

1/4 teaspoon salt, or to taste

1/8 teaspoon ground red pepper (optional)

1 In a 3-quart saucepan, heat the oil over medium-high heat. Stir in the onion and apples; cook until onions are transparent and apples are softened, about 3 minutes. Stir in the curry, coriander, ginger, cardamom, and turmeric until the spices are absorbed.

2 Stir in the crushed tomatoes, broth, and water. Bring to a boil. Reduce heat and simmer, uncovered, 40 minutes. Stir in the brown sugar, salt, and pepper.

3 Place half of the soup in a blender or food processor. Cover and puree. Repeat with remaining soup.

SWEET-AND-SOUR CABBAGE SOUP

MAKES 6 1/2 CUPS • SERVES 6 TO 8

If you're into fusion cooking, add some chopped cilantro just before serving for an unusual twist on this old Eastern European favorite.

2 tablespoons vegetable oil
2 cups shredded cabbage
1 1/2 cups sliced celery
1 cup sliced onion
2 cloves garlic, minced
6 cups water
One 6-ounce can tomato paste
1/4 cup firmly packed light or dark brown sugar
2 tablespoons white vinegar
1/4 teaspoon salt, or to taste
1/4 teaspoon ground black pepper

1 In a 4-quart saucepan, heat the oil over medium-high heat. Stir in the cabbage, celery, onion, and garlic; cook, stirring, until onion is transparent and cabbage is softened, about 5 minutes.

2 Stir in the water, tomato paste, brown sugar, vinegar, salt, and pepper. Bring to a boil. Reduce heat and simmer, uncovered, 50 minutes or until vegetables are tender.

VARIATION Add 1 cup sauerkraut when you add the water.

SQUASH AND APPLE SOUP

MAKES 5 CUPS • SERVES 4 TO 6

This very smooth soup is good for Thanksgiving if you want a change from pumpkin soup. My family won't let me come to the celebration without it! Like many soups, you can vary this recipe by adding a little curry powder when you add the ginger and nutmeg.

2 teaspoons vegetable oil
1 1/2 cups peeled, chopped apples
3/4 cup chopped onion
1/4 teaspoon ground ginger
1/8 teaspoon ground nutmeg
2 cups vegetable broth (homemade, page 158,
　or store-bought)
1 cup water
2 cups peeled, cubed butternut or buttercup squash
1/8 teaspoon salt, or to taste
1/8 teaspoon ground red pepper

1 In a 3-quart saucepan, heat the oil over medium-high heat. Add the apples and onion; cook, stirring, until softened, about 4 minutes. Stir in the ginger and nutmeg until absorbed. Add the broth and water; bring to a boil. Add the squash and return to a boil. Reduce heat and simmer, uncovered, 30 minutes or until vegetables are tender.

2 Place half of the soup in a blender or food processor. Cover and puree until smooth. Repeat with remaining soup, salt, and red pepper. Return soup to pot and reheat if necessary.

VARIATION For a richer, creamier soup, add 1/2 cup half-and-half after you've pureed the soup.

SOUPS

FRENCH ONION SOUP

MAKES 6 BOWLS • SERVES 6

I used to try to make this soup with shredded cheese and the cheese always ended up at the bottom of the bowl. By hanging the edges of a slice of cheese over the rim of the bowl, the cheese stays afloat. Make the onion soup ahead of time, then reheat, but don't add the bread and cheese until just before serving.

2 tablespoons butter or margarine
4 cups sliced mild onions
6 cups vegetable broth (homemade, page 158, or store-bought)
1/4 cup dry red wine
3 tablespoons dry sherry
1/2 teaspoon dried thyme
1/4 teaspoon dried savory
1/8 teaspoon salt, or to taste
1/8 teaspoon ground black pepper
1 bay leaf
6 slices day-old French bread
6 tablespoons grated Parmesan cheese, divided
Eight 1-ounce slices Swiss cheese

1 In a 3-quart saucepan melt the butter or margarine over medium-high heat. Add the onions; cook, stirring, until onions are very soft but not browned, about 5 minutes.

2 Stir in broth, wine, sherry, thyme, savory, salt, pepper, and bay leaf; bring to a boil. Reduce heat and simmer, uncovered, 50 minutes. Discard the bay leaf.

3 Preheat broiler.

4 Spoon 1 cup of soup into each of 4 ovenproof soup crocks. Float 1 slice of bread over the soup in each crock. Sprinkle 1 tablespoon of the Parmesan cheese over the bread and soup in each crock. Arrange the slices of Swiss cheese over the soup, so that the cheese hangs slightly over the edge of the crock.

5 Broil, 4 inches from the heat source, 4 to 5 minutes, or until the cheese is melted and bubbly.

VARIATION Use Melba toast rounds if you don't have French bread on hand. If the French bread is not stale, toast it until just lightly browned.

VEGAN VARIATION Serve the soup after step 2.

100 BEST VEGETARIAN RECIPES

EGG DROP VEGETABLE SOUP

MAKES 4 CUPS • SERVES 4

My tasters all had seconds of this soup—I'd say that's a pretty high recommendation. If you are concerned about cholesterol, use two egg whites instead of 1 whole egg. Make this soup without the egg and you have a tasty vegan Asian Vegetable Soup

1 1/2 cups water

4 dried shiitake mushrooms

1 1/2 cups vegetable broth (homemade, page 158, or store-bought)

1 tablespoon cornstarch

1 1/2 teaspoons soy sauce, or to taste

1/4 cup julienned carrots

1 egg, beaten (optional)

1 cup diced tofu (about 6 ounces)

1 cup shredded fresh spinach

1/2 cup sliced, canned bamboo shoots

2 tablespoons thinly sliced scallions (green part only)

1 In a 2-quart saucepan, bring the water to a boil over high heat. Remove from heat, add mushrooms, and let stand 10 minutes or until mushrooms are soft. Remove mushrooms from pot and slice. Reserve soaking liquid in pot.

2 In a medium bowl, stir together the vegetable broth, cornstarch, and soy sauce. Add the broth mixture, sliced mushrooms, and carrots to the mushroom water in the pot. Bring to a boil, stirring constantly. While stirring, gradually add the egg to the soup, if desired. Stir in the tofu, spinach, bamboo shoots, and scallions.

3 Simmer until the spinach is cooked and the tofu is heated through, about 5 minutes.

VARIATION Add 1/3 cup cooked fresh or frozen peas when you add the tofu.

VEGAN VARIATION Omit the egg.

CORN CHOWDER

MAKES 4 3/4 CUPS • SERVES 4 TO 6

If you use canned corn, add the canning liquid to the soup for extra flavor.

2 tablespoons butter or margarine
1 cup chopped onion
1 cup chopped celery
3 tablespoons all-purpose flour
3 cups vegetable broth (homemade, page 158, or store-bought)
1 cup peeled, diced potatoes (cut into 1/2-inch pieces)
2 cups corn kernels (fresh; canned, drained; or frozen)
1/8 teaspoon dried thyme
1 bay leaf
1/3 cup heavy cream
1/4 teaspoon ground black pepper
1/8 teaspoon salt, or to taste

1 In a 3-quart saucepan, melt the butter or margarine. Stir in the onion and celery; cook, stirring, until softened, about 3 minutes. Add the flour and stir until absorbed.

2 Add the broth and bring to a boil, stirring occasionally. Add the potatoes, corn, thyme, and bay leaf; return to a boil. Reduce heat and simmer, uncovered, stirring occasionally, 15 minutes or until the potatoes are tender. Discard bay leaf.

3 Stir in the cream, pepper, and salt. Continue to cook, stirring, until heated through.

VEGAN VARIATION Use additional broth instead of the cream.

MULLIGATAWNY SOUP

MAKES 5 1/2 CUPS • SERVES 4 TO 6

I always order this Anglo-Indian dish when I am dining in an Indian restaurant. Although the name is derived from the Tamil word for pepper water, it's not an overly spicy soup. It's amazing how differently it is interpreted from one restaurant to the next. This version stands up with the best of them.

2 tablespoons butter or margarine
1/2 cup finely chopped onion
1/4 cup finely chopped red bell pepper
1 1/2 cups peeled, chopped tart apples, plus more for garnish
1/2 cup finely chopped carrot
1/2 cup finely chopped celery
2 tablespoons all-purpose flour
1 tablespoon curry powder
2 cups vegetable broth (homemade, page 158,
   or store-bought)
2 cups water
3/4 cup unsweetened coconut milk (homemade, page 163,
   or store-bought)
1/4 cup white rice
1 tablespoon fresh lemon juice
1/4 teaspoon salt, or to taste
1/8 teaspoon ground red pepper
1 tablespoon chopped fresh cilantro or parsley (optional)

1 In a 3-quart saucepan, melt the butter or margarine over medium-high heat. Add the onion and bell pepper; cook, stirring, until softened, about 2 minutes. Add the apples, carrot, and celery; cook, stirring, until softened, about 3 minutes.

2 Stir in the flour and curry powder until absorbed.

3 Add the broth, water, coconut milk, and rice. Bring to a boil. Reduce heat and simmer, uncovered, 20 minutes or until rice is tender.

4 Stir in lemon juice, salt, and red pepper; simmer 5 minutes. Stir in cilantro, if desired. Sprinkle with chopped apples and serve.

VARIATION For a lighter soup, omit the rice. For a thicker, heartier version, puree the soup after cooking.

LENTIL SPINACH SOUP

MAKES 8 CUPS • SERVES 8 TO 10

This is a hearty, nutritious, and delicious soup. If you like escarole, it's excellent here; use 4 cups chopped in place of the spinach. If you do not want to use bouillon cubes, substitute quality boxed or canned vegetable broth or even homemade broth (page 158) for 4 cups of the water. Poultry seasoning is a mixture of herbs, usually containing sage, that can be found in the spice section of your supermarket.

1 cup lentils

8 cups water

1 cup chopped carrots

1 cup chopped celery

1 cup chopped onion

1/4 cup chopped fresh celery leaves

1 bay leaf

4 cups coarsely chopped fresh spinach (or 1 package frozen)

1/2 cup chopped fresh basil or 2 teaspoons dried basil

1 teaspoon celery salt

1 clove garlic, minced

1/2 teaspoon poultry seasoning

1/4 teaspoon ground black pepper

1 to 2 vegetable bouillon cubes, or 2 teaspoons vegetable bouillon powder (optional)

1 Rinse the lentils and discard any foreign matter.

2 In a 4-quart pot, bring the water to a boil over high heat. Add the lentils, carrots, celery, onion, celery leaves, and bay leaf; bring to a boil. Reduce heat and simmer, uncovered, 50 minutes, or until lentils are tender; discard the bay leaf.

3 Stir in the spinach, basil, celery salt, garlic, poultry seasoning, and pepper. Let simmer 10 minutes longer. Stir in bouillon, if desired.

VARIATION Omit the basil; stir in 1 teaspoon dried oregano instead.

SPICED INDIAN SPLIT PEA SOUP

MAKES 2 1/4 CUPS • SERVES 2 TO 3 AS A SOUP OR 4 TO 6 AS A SIDE DISH

This soup, also known as dal, is a traditional Indian dish, usually made with red lentils. It's not really a soup, but is used as a condiment with entrées. The consistency, however, is really that of a thick pea soup, and it does make a great untraditional first course.

1 tablespoon vegetable oil
1/2 cup chopped onion
1 teaspoon ground coriander
1/2 teaspoon cumin seed or 1/4 teaspoon ground cumin
1/2 teaspoon ground turmeric
5 cups water
3/4 cup yellow split peas
1 bay leaf
1/2 teaspoon salt, or to taste

1 In a 2-quart saucepan, heat the oil over medium-high heat. Add the onion; cook, stirring, until softened, about 2 minutes. Stir in the coriander, cumin seed, and turmeric until spices are absorbed and the seeds are coated with oil.

2 Add the water and bring to a boil. Stir in the split peas and bay leaf; return to a boil. Reduce heat and simmer, uncovered, 1 hour and 15 minutes or until the split peas are soft and have broken down. Discard the bay leaf. Stir in the salt.

SOUPS

MUSHROOM BARLEY SOUP

MAKES 6 CUPS • SERVES 6 TO 8

This is a very vegetable-rich soup—a real favorite in my family. Try to find dark, imported dried mushrooms. The ones from Poland are the best, but also extremely expensive. South American dried mushrooms, available in small plastic containers in the supermarket, are also good and not too expensive.

6 cups water, divided
1/2 ounce dried mushrooms (see headnote)
1 tablespoon vegetable oil
2 cups sliced white mushrooms
1 1/2 cups chopped onions
1 cup diced carrots
1 cup diced celery
1 cup peeled, diced parsnips
1/4 cup pearl barley
1/3 cup chopped fresh parsley
1/3 cup snipped fresh dill
1/4 teaspoon salt, or to taste
1/4 teaspoon ground black pepper

1 In a small saucepan, bring 1/2 cup of the water to a boil. Add the dried mushrooms and let stand 10 minutes or until softened. Chop mushrooms; set aside and reserve the soaking liquid.

2 In a 4-quart saucepan, heat the oil over medium-high heat. Add the white mushrooms and onions; cook, stirring, until softened, about 3 to 5 minutes.

3 Add the remaining water and the carrots, celery, parsnips, barley, and reserved chopped mushrooms and liquid; bring to a boil. Reduce heat and simmer, uncovered, 30 minutes. Add the parsley, dill, salt, and pepper. Simmer 15 minutes longer.

VARIATION Add 1 cup peeled, diced potatoes when you add the herbs.

LO LACTO-OVO **L** LACTO **V** VEGAN ✳ VEGAN VARIATION **M** MAKE-AHEAD

ESCAROLE BEAN SOUP

MAKES 8 CUPS • SERVES 8 TO 10

I first tasted this divine soup in a local pizzeria. It takes only 20 minutes to prepare. I have lots of friends who use this recipe, and they offer these suggestions. Double the recipe so you can use the entire head of escarole and freeze any leftovers. You can substitute frozen spinach for the escarole. That way, you can always have the ingredients for this soup on hand.

2 teaspoons vegetable oil

3/4 cup chopped onion

1 clove garlic, minced

One 14 1/2-ounce can whole peeled tomatoes, undrained

4 cups vegetable broth (homemade, page 158, or store-bought)

4 cups lightly packed, bite-size pieces escarole

1 cup cooked cannellini beans (cooked from dry; or canned, drained)

1/4 cup small bow-tie pasta (or other small pasta, such as orzo) (optional)

1 teaspoon sugar

1/2 teaspoon dried oregano

1 In a 3-quart saucepan, heat the oil over medium-high heat. Add the onion and garlic; cook, stirring, until softened, about 2 minutes. Add the tomatoes with liquid and break them up with the back of a spoon.

2 Add the broth and bring to a boil. Add the remaining ingredients; return to a boil. Reduce heat and simmer, uncovered, 10 minutes or until pasta is tender.

VARIATION Use kidney beans or chickpeas instead of the cannellini beans.

CHILLED CUCUMBER SOUP

MAKES 3 1/2 CUPS • SERVES 4

Summer days and cucumber soup were made for each other. When I'm feeling decadent I make this soup with heavy cream in place of some of the buttermilk. I find the blender works better for preparing this soup than the food processor.

2 medium peeled, seeded cucumbers, coarsely chopped
3 medium scallions, coarsely chopped
1 cup vegetable broth (homemade, page 158, or store-bought)
6 sprigs fresh dill or 1/2 teaspoon dried dill
1 cup buttermilk
1/4 teaspoon anchovy-free Worcestershire sauce
1/4 teaspoon salt, or to taste
1/8 teaspoon freshly ground black pepper

Place the cucumbers, scallions, vegetable broth, and dill in a blender. Cover and puree. Add the buttermilk, Worcestershire sauce, salt, and pepper. Cover and blend until combined. Chill. Add scallion, avocado, or cucumber chunks for garnish, if desired.

VARIATION Substitute fresh cilantro for the dill.

VEGAN VARIATION Use additional broth instead of the buttermilk.

GAZPACHO

MAKES 3 CUPS • SERVES 3 TO 4

This gazpacho is more of a rust color than the red that immediately comes to mind in most soups made with canned tomato juice. You may have to process this in two batches.

4 cups tomato wedges

1 cup peeled cucumber chunks

1/2 cup green bell pepper chunks

1 whole medium scallion

2 tablespoons red wine vinegar

2 teaspoons olive oil

1 clove garlic, minced

1/4 teaspoon salt, or to taste

Place all the ingredients in a blender or food processor. Cover and puree. Chill.

VARIATION For a spicier version, add 1/2 jalapeño pepper or 1/8 to 1/4 teaspoon ground red pepper.

LO LACTO-OVO L LACTO V VEGAN ✳ VEGAN VARIATION M MAKE-AHEAD

VICHYSSOISE

MAKES 4 1/2 CUPS • SERVES 4 TO 6

Traditionally served chilled, vichyssoise is also perfectly delicious warm, in which case it's called Potato-Leek Soup (see variation). It's nice to use white pepper in this recipe so you don't have black specks in the otherwise cream-colored soup, but if you don't have any white pepper, the black will taste just fine. For a decadent soup, substitute heavy cream for some or all of the half-and-half.

2 tablespoons butter or margarine
1 1/2 cups sliced leeks (white and light green parts)
3 cups vegetable broth (homemade, page 158, or store-bought)
2 cups peeled potatoes, cut into 1-inch cubes
1/2 cup half-and-half
1/8 teaspoon ground white pepper
Snipped fresh chives, for garnish

1 In a 2-quart saucepan, melt the butter or margarine over medium-high heat. Add the leeks; cook, stirring, until softened, about 1 minute.

2 Add the broth and bring to a boil. Add the potatoes; reduce heat and simmer, uncovered, 25 minutes or until potatoes are tender.

3 Place half of the soup in a blender or food processor. Cover and puree until smooth. Repeat with remaining soup. Add half-and-half and pepper. Chill.

4 Serve garnished with fresh chives.

VARIATION Potato-Leek Soup: Serve warm, reheating if necessary after adding the half-and-half.

VEGAN VARIATION Omit the half-and-half; substitute either unsweetened soy milk or additional broth.

LO LACTO-OVO L LACTO V VEGAN ✱ VEGAN VARIATION M MAKE-AHEAD

ENTRÉES

CREOLE RED BEANS AND RICE

MAKES 5 1/2 CUPS • SERVES 4 TO 6

The type of bean you use does not really affect the final dish, although some types may take longer than others to cook. Just keep tasting until the beans are soft.

1 cup dry red, pinto, black, or kidney beans
1 tablespoon vegetable oil
1 cup chopped onion
1 cup chopped celery
1 cup chopped green bell peppers, divided
3 cloves garlic, minced, divided
1 teaspoon chili powder
2 cups water
One 14 1/2-ounce can whole peeled tomatoes, undrained
1/2 teaspoon salt, or to taste
4 cups cooked white or brown rice

1 Place the beans in a 1 1/2-quart saucepan; cover with water. Bring to a boil over medium heat; boil 2 minutes. Remove from heat and let stand 1 hour. Drain.

2 In a 3-quart saucepan, heat the oil over medium-high heat. Add the onion, celery, bell peppers, and garlic. Cook, stirring, until softened, about 3 minutes. Stir in chili powder until absorbed. Add water and beans; bring to a boil. Reduce heat and simmer, covered, 1 1/2 hours or until beans are tender.

3 Add the tomatoes and salt; break up the tomatoes with the back of a spoon. Simmer, covered, 25 minutes longer. Serve over cooked rice.

VARIATION Add ground red pepper to taste.

BLACK BEAN–POLENTA PIE

MAKES ONE 9-INCH PIE • SERVES 6

In order to form a smooth crust, the polenta has to be freshly cooked and spread in the pie plate as soon as it has finished cooking. Try to make the edge of the crust a little higher than the sides of the dish.

2 1/2 cups cooked polenta (page 160)
1 tablespoon vegetable oil
1 cup chopped onion
1 cup chopped green bell peppers
1 cup chopped canned tomatoes, or one 8-ounce can whole peeled tomatoes, undrained
1 1/2 cups cooked black beans (cooked from dry; or canned, drained)
1 cup cooked corn kernels (fresh; canned, drained; or frozen)
One 4-ounce can chopped chiles, drained
1 1/2 cups shredded Cheddar cheese, divided
1 egg
1/3 cup sour cream

1 Preheat the oven to 375°F.

2 Thickly spread the polenta into a greased 9-inch pie plate, making a high crust over the edge of the dish.

3 In a large skillet, heat the oil over medium-high heat. Add the onion and bell peppers; cook, stirring, until tender, about 3 minutes. Add the tomatoes; cook, stirring, until most of the liquid has evaporated. Stir in the beans, corn, and chiles. Stir in 1 cup of the Cheddar cheese.

4 In a small bowl, beat the egg; beat in the sour cream. Add to the bean mixture and stir until combined. Spoon into the polenta shell. Top with the remaining cheese. Bake 35 minutes or until bean mixture has heated through and cheese has melted.

VARIATION Substitute plain yogurt for the sour cream.

ENTRÉES

SOUTHWESTERN STEW

MAKES 3 3/4 CUPS • SERVES 4

I add the carrots toward the end of cooking time so they retain some of their crunchiness. If you prefer soft carrots, add them when you add the beans.

1 tablespoon vegetable oil
1 cup chopped bell peppers
3 cloves garlic, minced
1 tablespoon chili powder
1/4 teaspoon ground cumin
1/4 teaspoon ground cinnamon
One 14 1/4-ounce can whole peeled tomatoes, undrained
1 1/2 cups cooked black beans (cooked from dry; or canned, drained)
1 cup corn kernels (fresh; frozen; or canned, drained)
1/4 cup water
1 teaspoon sugar
1/4 teaspoon ground sage
1/4 teaspoon salt, or to taste
1/4 teaspoon hot sauce (optional)
1 cup diced carrots
1/3 cup chopped fresh cilantro

1 In a 3-quart pot, heat the oil over medium-high heat. Add bell peppers and garlic. Cook, stirring, until the vegetables are softened, about 2 minutes. Stir in the chili powder, cumin, and cinnamon.

2 Add the tomatoes, breaking them up with the back of a spoon. Add the black beans, corn, water, sugar, sage, salt, and hot sauce. Cook, uncovered, stirring occasionally, for 15 minutes. Stir in the carrots and cilantro. Cook, uncovered, 10 minutes longer or until vegetables are tender and stew is slightly thickened.

VARIATION Substitute 1 cup diced zucchini for the carrots or add it with the carrots.

BROWN RICE AND BLACK BEAN BURRITOS

MAKES 4 BURRITOS • SERVES 4 TO 6

You can prepare these burritos using store-bought or homemade salsa (page 162) and/or guacamole (page 28). I usually cut these burritos in half because they can be too big for some people. Or, instead of making giant burritos, you can use smaller tortillas and make 6 smaller burritos.

4 large (10-inch) flour tortillas

1/3 cup finely chopped, seeded tomatoes

3 tablespoons minced onion

2 tablespoons minced bell pepper

2 cups cooked brown rice

1 cup cooked black beans (cooked from dry; or canned, drained)

1/2 cup mild or medium salsa

1/2 cup shredded Monterey Jack cheese

1 cup guacamole

1 Preheat the oven to 350°F. Wrap the tortillas in foil and place in oven; heat about 5 to 10 minutes or until tortillas are warm and pliable.

2 While the tortillas are heating, combine the tomatoes, onion, and bell pepper in a small bowl; set aside.

3 In a 1-quart saucepan, stir together the brown rice, beans, and salsa. Cook over low heat until heated through, about 4 minutes.

4 Remove the tortillas from the oven. Place one on a serving plate. Place 1/4 of the bean mixture (a generous 1/2 cup) in the center of the tortilla. Top with 2 tablespoons shredded cheese, 1/4 cup guacamole, and 1/4 of the tomato mixture.

5 Fold two opposite sides of the tortilla over the filling. Lift the edge of one of the remaining sides; fold it over filling and roll to form a wide log. Repeat with remaining tortillas and filling.

VARIATION Substitute Cheddar cheese for the Monterey Jack.

VEGAN VARIATION Omit the cheese completely.

ENTRÉES

CHILI

MAKES 4 2/3 CUPS • SERVES 4 TO 6

Maybe I'm biased, but I think this is one of the best vegetarian chili recipes I've ever tasted. Others agree! Serve topped with sour cream or plain yogurt, and/or chopped onion or scallions, and/or shredded Cheddar cheese.

2 tablespoons vegetable oil
2 cups chopped onions
6 cloves garlic, minced
1/4 cup chili powder
1 tablespoon paprika
1 teaspoon ground cumin
1 teaspoon dried oregano
4 cups chopped tomatoes
1 bay leaf
1/2 teaspoon sugar
1/2 teaspoon salt, or to taste
1/8 teaspoon ground red pepper (optional)
3 cups cooked kidney beans (cooked from dry; or canned, drained)

1 In a 4-quart saucepan, heat the oil over medium-high heat. Add the onions and garlic; cook, stirring, until softened, about 2 minutes. Stir in the chili powder, paprika, cumin, and oregano until absorbed.

2 Stir in the tomatoes, bay leaf, sugar, salt, and red pepper; bring to a boil. Reduce heat and simmer, covered, 20 minutes, stirring occasionally.

3 Add the beans; simmer, covered, 15 to 20 minutes longer or until chili is slightly thick, stirring occasionally. Discard the bay leaf.

VARIATION Add 1 cup chopped green bell peppers when you add the onions.

100 BEST VEGETARIAN RECIPES

FAJITAS

MAKES 8 FAJITAS • SERVES 4

You can serve these vegetables over rice instead of rolled in tortillas.

1 tablespoon vegetable oil
1 tablespoon fresh lime juice
1 teaspoon chili powder
1 teaspoon dried oregano
1/4 teaspoon ground cumin
2 large cloves garlic, minced
1/8 teaspoon salt, or to taste
6 cups vegetables cut into strips (such as bell peppers, Portobello mushrooms, zucchini, yellow squash, carrots, or eggplant)
Eight 7-inch flour tortillas
1/2 cup salsa (homemade, page 162, or store-bought)

1 In a large bowl, stir together the oil, lime juice, chili powder, oregano, cumin, garlic, and salt. Add the vegetables and toss to coat; let marinate at least 1 hour.

2 Preheat the broiler. Line a pan with foil; cook vegetables until desired doneness, turning once.

3 Warm the tortillas on the grill or in the oven. Place 1/2 cup of the vegetables in the center of each tortilla, top each with 1 tablespoon salsa. Fold one side over the vegetables, then roll to form a tube.

VARIATION Top vegetables with 2 tablespoons guacamole (you'll need 1 cup total for the recipe) before adding the salsa.

CURRIED SPINACH–STUFFED PEPPERS

MAKES 4 HALVES • SERVES 4

These peppers are stuffed with a delicious curried spinach with orzo. If you would like to make the filling more substantial, add more orzo to taste.

2 large or 4 small red or green bell peppers

CURRIED SPINACH
2 tablespoons water

2 teaspoons minced fresh ginger

2 cloves garlic

1 dried hot pepper or 1/2 teaspoon crushed red pepper, or to taste

1 teaspoon ground coriander

1 teaspoon cumin seed or 1 teaspoon ground cumin

1 teaspoon paprika

1/2 teaspoon ground turmeric

1/2 teaspoon salt, or to taste

2 tablespoons ghee (page 90) or vegetable oil

Two 10-ounce packages frozen chopped spinach, thawed and slightly drained

1/4 cup cooked orzo or other small pasta

1/4 cup unsweetened coconut milk (homemade, page 163, or store-bought)

1 Preheat the oven to 375°F.

2 If using large bell peppers, cut them in half through the stem, discard seeds and pith; or, if using small peppers, cut off the top with the stem, then remove seeds and pith. Blanch in boiling water 4 minutes; drain. Set aside.

3 Place the water, ginger, garlic, pepper, coriander, cumin seed, paprika, turmeric, and salt into a blender container. Cover and blend until a paste forms.

4 In a large skillet, heat the ghee over medium-high heat. Add the spice puree to the pan. Cook until heated. Stir in the spinach, then the orzo and coconut milk. Cook 5 minutes or until heated through.

100 BEST VEGETARIAN RECIPES

5 Spoon 1/4 of the mixture into each of the prepared pepper shells.

6 Place the stuffed peppers in a 9-inch square pan. Bake 25 minutes or until filling is heated through.

CURRIED CHICKPEAS AND KALE

MAKES 4 1/2 CUPS • SERVES 4

This rich, flavorful curry is so satisfying. It uses ghee, the Indian version of clarified butter, which means the milk solids have been removed. Because there is no milk in the ghee, it can be stored, covered, at room temperature without spoiling for a few months. It is the preferred fat for cooking Indian food, but you can substitute butter or vegetable oil if you don't want to bother making or purchasing ghee.

2 tablespoons ghee (see below) or vegetable oil
1 1/2 cups chopped onions
4 cloves garlic, minced
1/2 teaspoon cumin seed
3 cups chopped kale
1 1/2 tablespoons curry powder
1 teaspoon ground ginger
1 teaspoon ground coriander
1 1/2 cups vegetable broth (homemade, page 158, or store-bought)
3 cups cooked chickpeas (cooked from dry; or canned, drained)
1 cup chopped tomatoes
1/4 teaspoon salt, or to taste

1 In a 2-quart saucepan, heat the ghee or oil over medium-high heat. Add the onions, garlic, and cumin; cook, stirring, until softened, about 2 minutes. Add the kale; cook, stirring, until softened, about 2 minutes more.

2 Stir in the curry powder, ginger, and coriander. Add the broth and bring to a boil. Add the chickpeas, tomatoes, and salt; return to a boil. Reduce heat and simmer, uncovered, 25 minutes.

VARIATION Substitute Swiss chard or one 10-ounce package frozen chopped spinach for the kale.

TO MAKE GHEE Place 1 cup unsalted butter in a heavy 1-quart saucepan. Cook over medium-low heat until the butter starts to boil; continue cooking, uncovered, until the sizzling sounds stop and the solids on the bottom turn brown, about 8 minutes. Remove from heat and let stand 10 minutes. Strain through a fine sieve to remove any milk solids.

OKRA, PLANTAIN, AND SWEET POTATO CURRY

V
M

MAKES 5 CUPS • SERVES 5 TO 6

I think of this as a Caribbean curry, because many of these ingredients are native to tropical regions of the world. Now, thanks to good shipping methods, they are available practically anywhere. If the okra are small, use them whole; otherwise, cut them in half or slice them. The lemongrass is tough to chew but adds great flavor. If you can't find lemongrass, add 1 teaspoon grated lemon zest instead. To peel the plantain more easily, cut into slices before peeling.

2 tablespoons vegetable oil
1 1/2 cups sliced onion (1/4 inch thick)
1 clove garlic, minced
1 1/2 tablespoons curry powder
1 teaspoon paprika
1/2 teaspoon ground cardamom
1/4 teaspoon ground cinnamon
2 cups water
3/4 cup unsweetened coconut milk (homemade, page 163, or store-bought)
2 cups peeled, cubed sweet potatoes
2 cups sliced, peeled green plantains
2 teaspoons dried lemongrass
1/2 teaspoon dried basil
2 cups whole okra, tops trimmed
2 tablespoons chopped fresh cilantro
1/4 teaspoon salt, or to taste

1 In a 3-quart saucepan, heat the oil over medium-high heat. Add the onion and garlic; cook, stirring, until softened, about 2 minutes. Stir in the curry powder, paprika, cardamom, and cinnamon.

2 Add the water and coconut milk; bring to a boil. Add the sweet potatoes, plantains, lemongrass, and basil; return to a boil. Reduce heat and simmer, uncovered, 40 minutes. Add the okra, cilantro, and salt; return to a boil. Simmer, uncovered, 10 minutes or until okra are tender.

VARIATION Add 1 cup peas when you add the okra.

ENTRÉES

MACARONI AND THREE CHEESES

MAKES 7 CUPS • SERVES 4 TO 6

This is definitely an American classic. Some kids who have grown up with packaged versions may be disappointed with the real thing, but adults will love this very creamy comfort food.

12 ounces elbow macaroni
1/4 cup butter or margarine
1/4 cup all-purpose flour
3 cups milk
1 1/2 cups shredded Cheddar cheese
1 cup shredded Gouda
1/2 cup shredded mozzarella cheese
1/4 teaspoon anchovy-free Worcestershire sauce
1/4 teaspoon salt, or to taste
Plain, dry bread crumbs (optional)

1 Preheat the oven to 350°F.

2 Cook the macaroni according to package directions for the minimum suggested time so that pasta is just al dente; drain.

3 In a 3-quart saucepan, melt the butter or margarine over medium-high heat. Stir in the flour until absorbed.

4 Using a whisk, stir in the milk. Cook over medium heat, stirring constantly, until mixture comes to a boil (make sure you get all the edges of the pot so that there are no clumps in the bottom). Stir in all cheeses, the Worcestershire sauce, and salt. Remove from heat and continue stirring until cheeses are melted. Stir in the cooked macaroni. Pour into a greased 9-inch square baking pan. Sprinkle with bread crumbs, if desired.

5 Bake 30 to 45 minutes or until top is browned and mixture is heated through and bubbly.

VARIATION Good Old Macaroni and Cheese: Use an additional 1 1/2 cups of shredded Cheddar cheese instead of the Gouda and mozzarella cheese.

LO LACTO-OVO   **L** LACTO   **V** VEGAN   **✳** VEGAN VARIATION   **M** MAKE-AHEAD

PENNE WITH VODKA SAUCE

MAKES 7 CUPS • SERVES 4 TO 6

If you don't have vodka on hand, you can use gin or even white wine. If you prefer not to use alcohol, you can substitute broth, but it's not quite the same without the vodka. You can make the sauce ahead of time, but don't combine it with the pasta until just before serving.

1 tablespoon olive oil

1 cup chopped onion

2 cloves garlic, minced

One 14 1/2-ounce can whole peeled tomatoes, undrained

1/4 cup vodka

3 tablespoons tomato paste

1 1/2 teaspoons sugar

1/4 teaspoon salt, or to taste

1/8 teaspoon crushed red pepper

12 ounces penne pasta

1/4 cup heavy cream

1 In a 1 1/2 quart saucepan, heat the oil over medium-high heat. Add the onion and garlic; cook, stirring, until softened, about 2 minutes.

2 Add the tomatoes and break them up with the back of a spoon. Stir in the vodka, tomato paste, sugar, salt, and red pepper. Cook, uncovered, over medium heat 20 minutes, stirring occasionally.

3 While the sauce is cooking, cook the pasta according to package directions; drain.

4 Stir the cream into the sauce; cook, stirring, until heated through. Do not allow to boil. Pour sauce over pasta and toss.

VARIATION Stir in 1/4 to 1/3 cup grated Parmesan cheese when you add the cream.

VEGAN VARIATION Omit the cream for a lighter sauce.

PASTA PUTTANESCA

MAKES 3 1/2 CUPS SAUCE • SERVES 3 TO 4

I tested this recipe using 12 ounces of thin spaghetti and, although the flavor was very good, I really like my pasta dishes saucier, so I reduced the amount of pasta to 8 ounces. If you like your pasta less saucy, you can serve this sauce on 12 ounces of pasta. As with the Penne with Vodka Sauce (page 94), you can prepare this sauce ahead of time, but don't combine it with the pasta until you are ready to serve.

1 1/2 tablespoons olive oil
1 cup chopped onion
3 cloves garlic, minced
One 14 1/2-ounce can whole peeled tomatoes, undrained
1/2 cup water
1/3 cup chopped oil-marinated sun-dried tomatoes
1/4 cup tomato paste
1 1/2 teaspoons sugar
1/8 teaspoon crushed red pepper
One 5.75-ounce can pitted black olives, drained and chopped
1/2 cup chopped fresh parsley
1 tablespoon chopped capers
8 to 12 ounces pasta (spaghetti, thin spaghetti, or linguine)

1 In a 2-quart saucepan, heat the oil over medium-high heat. Add the onion and garlic; cook, stirring, until softened, about 2 minutes.

2 Add the whole tomatoes, with liquid, and break them up with the back of a spoon. Stir in the water, sun-dried tomatoes, tomato paste, sugar, and red pepper flakes. Bring to a boil. Reduce heat and simmer, uncovered, 30 minutes or until thickened, stirring occasionally. Stir in the olives, parsley, and capers; cook until heated through, 2 minutes longer.

3 Cook the pasta according to package directions; drain. Either toss with sauce or serve topped with sauce.

VARIATION Add 1/3 cup chopped fresh basil when you add the olives, capers, and parsley.

ESCAROLE-STUFFED SHELLS

MAKES 20 JUMBO SHELLS • SERVES 4 TO 5

Even in a book called *100 Best Vegetarian Recipes*, this recipe is a standout. I find Fresh Tomato Sauce (page 161) to be especially wonderful with these shells, but you can use any marinara or similar homemade or store-bought sauce. If you don't want the starch of pasta, slice a medium eggplant lengthwise and grill according to instructions on page 159; roll the stuffing in the grilled eggplant slices.

1 tablespoon olive oil
1/4 cup finely chopped onion
1 clove garlic, minced
2 cups chopped escarole
1 1/2 cups ricotta cheese
1/2 cup shredded mozzarella cheese
1/4 cup grated Parmesan cheese
1/4 teaspoon salt, or to taste
1/8 teaspoon ground black pepper
20 jumbo pasta shells
3 1/2 to 4 cups tomato sauce (homemade, page 161, or store-bought)

1 Preheat the oven to 350°F.

2 In a medium skillet, heat the oil over medium-high heat. Add the onion and garlic; cook, stirring, until onions are softened, 1 to 2 minutes. Add the escarole; cook, stirring, until wilted, about 2 minutes. Cool.

3 In a medium bowl, stir together the ricotta, mozzarella, and Parmesan cheeses. Add the escarole mixture and salt and pepper.

4 Cook the shells according to package directions until just al dente. Drain and rinse in cool water, then drain again.

5 Stuff one heaping tablespoon of the cheese mixture into each of the shells.

6 Spread 2 to 3 cups of sauce over the bottom of a 9 x 13-inch baking pan. Arrange the shells in a single layer on the sauce. Pour the remaining sauce over the shells.

7 Bake 30 minutes or until the cheese is melted and the shells are heated through.

VARIATIONS Cheese-Stuffed Shells: Omit step 2 of the recipe, leaving out the olive oil, onion, garlic, and escarole. Stuffed Shells Parmigiana: Combine 1 cup of additional shredded mozzarella cheese plus 2 tablespoons additional grated Parmesan cheese. Sprinkle over the shells after you've added all the sauce.

ENTRÉES

EGGPLANT ROLLATINI

MAKES 12 ROLLATINI • SERVES 4 TO 6

You can salt and drain the eggplant slices before cooking if you like. Be sure to pat dry before frying.

SAUCE
1 tablespoon olive oil
3/4 cup chopped onion
2 cloves garlic, minced
One 14 1/2-ounce can whole peeled tomatoes, undrained
3 tablespoons tomato paste
1/4 teaspoon salt, or to taste
2/3 cup heavy cream

FILLING
One 15-ounce container ricotta cheese
1 cup shredded mozzarella cheese
1/4 cup chopped fresh parsley
3 tablespoons grated Parmesan cheese
1 clove garlic, minced
1/8 teaspoon ground pepper
Oil for frying (optional method)

2 to 3 medium eggplants, unpeeled (each about 7 inches long)

1 Preheat the oven to 375°F. To prepare the sauce, in a 2-quart saucepan, heat the 1 tablespoon oil over medium-high heat. Add the onion and 2 cloves minced garlic; cook, stirring, until softened, about 2 minutes. Add the tomatoes, with liquid, breaking them up with the back of a spoon. Stir in the tomato paste and 1/4 teaspoon salt. Bring to a boil. Reduce heat and simmer, uncovered, 20 minutes, stirring occasionally. Place sauce in a blender. (A blender is better than a food processor for this recipe, but if you only have a processor, that will do—just get the sauce as smooth as possible.) Cover and blend until smooth. Return to pot and stir in cream; set aside.

2 Meanwhile, for the filling, in a medium bowl, stir together the ricotta, mozzarella, parsley, Parmesan, 1 clove minced garlic, and the pepper; set aside.

3 Cut the eggplants lengthwise into 12 slices (1/8 to 1/4 inch thick). Discard the end slices that are mostly skin. Cook the eggplant slices by frying them in oil (which they soak up like a sponge) or broiling them (see page 159). The cooking method doesn't matter; it's just important that the eggplant be completely cooked, because it doesn't soften more in the baking.

4 Place 3 tablespoons of the filling on the thick end of each of the eggplant slices; roll to completely encase the filling.

5 Pour 1 cup of the sauce into the bottom of an 11 x 7 x 1 1/2-inch baking dish (or a 9-inch square baking dish). Place the rolls, seam down, into the dish. Top with the remaining sauce. Bake, uncovered, 15 minutes at 375°F, or until cheese is heated through and slightly runny.

VARIATION Broil the eggplant, omit the cream from the sauce (it tastes good even without the cream), and use part-skim ricotta and mozzarella.

RED, GREEN, AND WHITE LASAGNA

MAKES ONE 9 X 13-INCH LASAGNA • SERVES 8 TO 12

You can prepare the tomato sauce from scratch, or if you're in a hurry, use 4 cups of store-bought sauce. You can also add cooked vegetables to the filling for more variety. Add one or more of the following: eggplant, zucchini, yellow squash, carrots, or chopped bell peppers.

EASY TOMATO SAUCE
3 tablespoons olive oil
1 1/2 cups chopped onions
3 cloves garlic, minced
One 14 1/2-ounce can diced tomatoes, undrained
3/4 cup water
1/4 cup tomato paste
1/4 cup chopped parsley
1/4 teaspoon salt, or to taste
1/4 teaspoon ground pepper

FILLING
1/3 cup pine nuts *(pignoli)*
1 egg
One 15-ounce container ricotta cheese
2 cups shredded mozzarella, divided
1 1/2 cups shredded cheese (Fontina, Provolone, Asiago, or a combination of all three)
3/4 cup grated Parmesan cheese, divided
1/4 teaspoon ground pepper
Two 10-ounce packages frozen chopped spinach, thawed and squeezed dry

12 lasagna noodles

1 For the tomato sauce, in a 4-quart pot, heat the oil over medium-high heat. Add the onions and garlic; cook, stirring, until softened, about 2 minutes.

2 Add the remaining ingredients. Bring to a boil. Reduce heat to medium and cook, uncovered, 25 minutes or until thickened. Place plastic wrap on surface of sauce and set aside.

3 To begin the filling, over low heat, cook the pine nuts in a dry, small skillet until all the nuts are at least partially browned. Chop.

4 In a large bowl, heat the egg; stir in the ricotta and pine nuts. Add 1 cup of the mozzarella, the shredded cheese, 1/2 cup of the Parmesan, and pepper; stir to combine. Stir in the spinach.

5 Cook the noodles according to package directions; drain.

6 Preheat the oven to 375°F.

7 Thinly spread half of the tomato sauce in the bottom of a 9 x 13-inch baking dish. Use 4 of the noodles to line the bottom of the dish.

8 Spread 1/2 of the ricotta filling over the noodles.

9 Top with 4 more noodles. Spread with remaining ricotta filling.

10 Top with remaining noodles. Spread remaining sauce over noodles.

11 Bake 30 minutes. Sprinkle with remaining 1 cup mozzarella and 1/4 cup Parmesan; continue baking 20 minutes longer. Remove from oven and let stand 15 minutes before cutting into squares.

TORTELLINI WITH WILD MUSHROOM SAUCE

MAKES 2 CUPS SAUCE • SERVES 4 TO 6

You can also serve this sauce over gnocchi or plain pasta, such as penne or rigatoni.

1 1/2 tablespoons olive oil

2 tablespoons minced shallots

3 cups coarsely chopped wild mushrooms (such as Portobello, cremini, and/or shiitake)

1 1/2 cups vegetable broth (homemade, page 158, or store-bought)

1/2 cup water

2 tablespoons medium sweet Madeira or Marsala

1/4 teaspoon dried thyme

1/8 teaspoon salt, or to taste

1/8 teaspoon ground black pepper

2 tablespoons butter or margarine

3 tablespoons all-purpose flour

3 tablespoons heavy cream

2 tablespoons grated Parmesan cheese

1/4 cup chopped fresh parsley

Two 12-ounce packages fresh cheese tortellini

1 In a 2-quart saucepan, heat the oil over medium-high heat. Add the shallots; cook, stirring, until tender, about 30 seconds. Add the mushrooms; cook, stirring, until softened, about 4 minutes. Add the broth, water, Madeira, thyme, salt, and pepper. Bring to a boil. Reduce heat and simmer, uncovered, 10 minutes.

2 In a 1 1/2-quart saucepan, melt the butter or margarine over medium-high heat. Stir in the flour until absorbed. Stir in the mushroom mixture; cook, stirring, until mixture comes to a boil, about 2 minutes. Stir in the cream and Parmesan cheese. Add the parsley.

3 Cook the tortellini according to package directions; drain. Place in a large bowl, toss with the mushroom sauce, and serve.

VEGAN VARIATION Omit the heavy cream and cheese, and serve with mushroom-stuffed tortellini or ravioli, or with plain pasta.

ENTRÉES

SPAGHETTI SQUASH PROVENÇAL

MAKES 7 CUPS SQUASH AND 4 CUPS SAUCE • SERVES 4 TO 6

You can use spaghetti squash as you would pasta. Just cook the spaghetti squash as directed in step 1, then serve it topped with your favorite pasta sauce. If you want a "meaty" consistency to the sauce, stir in 3/4 cup rehydrated textured vegetable protein (TVP) or cooked bulgur (see page 169).

2 spaghetti squash (about 1 1/4 pounds each)
1 tablespoon olive oil
1 cup chopped onion
2 cloves garlic, minced
1/2 cup green bell pepper strips
1/2 cup red bell pepper strips
One 28-ounce can whole tomatoes in thick puree, undrained
1 1/2 cups sliced zucchini
1 1/2 cups sliced yellow squash
2 tablespoons Galliano, anisette, or orange liqueur (optional)
1/2 teaspoon dried basil
1/2 teaspoon dried rosemary, crumbled
1/2 teaspoon grated orange zest
1/4 teaspoon dried savory
1/4 teaspoon dried thyme
1/4 teaspoon salt, or to taste
1/4 teaspoon ground black pepper

1 Preheat the oven to 350°F. Bake the spaghetti squash 1 hour 15 minutes or until tender. Cut in half; discard seeds. Using a fork, scrape the flesh into a bowl, pulling into "spaghetti" strands.

2 Meanwhile, in a 3-quart saucepan, heat the oil over medium-high heat. Add the onion and garlic; cook, stirring, until onions are transparent, about 2 minutes. Stir in the bell peppers; cook, stirring, until softened, about 3 minutes.

3 Add the tomatoes and puree and break them up with the back of a spoon. Stir in the remaining ingredients.

4 Bring to a boil. Reduce heat and simmer, uncovered, 35 minutes or until sauce is thickened. Serve over spaghetti squash.

VARIATION Add 1 cup sliced carrots to the sauce when you add the zucchini.

EGGPLANT WITH RED PEPPERS AND SHIITAKE MUSHROOMS

MAKES 5 CUPS • SERVES 4

Port (wine) adds a deep richness to this sauce. If you do not have it, or Madeira, on hand, use 3 tablespoons of red wine combined with 1 tablespoon balsamic vinegar and 2 teaspoons sugar. I usually serve this over couscous, but it also makes a great sauce for pasta. I like to use it with penne, rigatoni, or similar medium-sized pasta.

2 tablespoons vegetable oil
2 cups sliced red bell peppers
1 cup chopped onion
1 clove garlic, minced
6 cups cubed eggplant (unpeeled)
2 cups coarsely chopped shiitake mushrooms
1 tablespoon all-purpose flour
1/2 cup vegetable broth (homemade, page 158, or store-bought)
1/4 cup port or Madeira
1 1/2 tablespoons dry sherry
1 tablespoon red wine vinegar
2 tablespoons chopped fresh parsley
1/8 teaspoon ground black pepper

1 In a large skillet, heat the oil over medium-high heat. Add the bell peppers, onion, and garlic; cook, stirring, until softened, about 3 minutes.

2 Add the eggplant and mushrooms; cook, stirring, until softened, about 3 minutes. Stir in the flour until absorbed.

3 Stir in the broth, port, sherry, and vinegar. Stir in the parsley and pepper. Cook, stirring, until mixture comes to a boil and sauce is thickened.

VARIATION Use green bell peppers instead of the red or sliced white mushrooms instead of the shiitake.

ENTRÉES

TUSCAN MUSHROOM AND POTATO TORTE

MAKES ONE 8-INCH PIE • SERVES 6

This very impressive entrée will be worth all the time and effort you put into it when you hear the oohs and aahs from your guests, but be sure to observe the standing time after baking. Cutting into the torte early will leave you with a runny mess.

OLIVE OIL PASTRY DOUGH (FOR TWO CRUSTS)
1 3/4 cups all-purpose flour
3/4 cup whole wheat flour
1 teaspoon salt
1/2 cup olive oil
1/3 to 1/2 cup ice water

MUSHROOM-POTATO FILLING
4 cups peeled, thinly sliced baking potatoes
2 tablespoons olive oil
2 cups sliced onions
3 cloves garlic, minced
3 cups sliced wild mushrooms (such as shiitake, Portobello, porcini, or cremini)
2 cups sliced white mushrooms
1/3 cup chopped fresh parsley
1/2 teaspoon dried sage leaves, crumbled
1 tablespoon butter or margarine
1 1/2 tablespoons all-purpose flour
1 cup vegetable broth (homemade, page 158, or store-bought)
1 teaspoon salt, or to taste
1/4 teaspoon ground black pepper

1 Preheat the oven to 350°F.

2 For the pastry dough, in a large bowl, stir together both flours and the salt. Stir in the oil and 3 tablespoons of the water. Add as much of the remaining water as necessary to form a stiff dough. Chill at least 30 minutes.

3 Divide dough into 2 pieces, one about 2/3 and the other 1/3 of the dough. Roll the larger piece into a 14-inch circle. Fit dough into the bottom and up the side of an 8-inch springform pan. Roll out the second piece of dough into a 9- to 10-inch circle; set aside.

4 For the filling, cook the potato slices in boiling water for 5 minutes; drain. Set aside.

5 In a large skillet, heat the oil over medium-high heat. Add the onions and garlic; cook, stirring until softened, about 2 minutes. Add mushrooms; cook, stirring, until softened, about 4 minutes. If mushrooms give off liquid, cook until it evaporates. Stir in parsley and sage.

6 In a 1-quart saucepan, melt the butter or margarine over medium-high heat. Stir in the flour until absorbed. Stir in the broth, salt, and pepper. Cook, stirring constantly, until mixture comes to a boil; set aside.

7 Layer 1/3 of the mushroom mixture in the bottom of the pastry. Top with 1/2 of the potatoes, to make a single overlapping layer. Top with half of the remaining mushrooms, then with remaining potatoes, then with remaining mushrooms. Pour sauce over the mushrooms.

8 Place second crust over mushrooms and make slits to vent. Seal edges by crimping the dough attractively.

9 Bake 1 hour 15 minutes or until crust is lightly browned. Let stand 20 minutes before serving.

VARIATION You can use dried oregano or basil or any other herb of your choice in place of the sage.

TOMATO-FETA TART

MAKES ONE 10-INCH TART • SERVES 6

The sliced tomatoes on top make this tart as attractive as it is tasty. However, the skin on the tomato can make it a little hard to slice into neat pieces. If you are feeling ambitious, you can skin the tomatoes before slicing. Dip into boiling water for 2 minutes, then plunge into ice water and peel off the skin.

Half-recipe of Olive Oil Pastry Dough (page 108), or one 9-inch frozen deep-dish crust

3 eggs

1 1/3 cups milk

1 clove garlic, minced

1/4 teaspoon salt, or to taste

1/4 teaspoon dried oregano

Dash Tabasco™

1 1/2 cups crumbled feta cheese (about 8 ounces)

15 thin slices red and yellow tomato (cut crosswise)

1 Preheat the oven to 375°F.

2 Roll the pastry into an 11-inch circle. Line a 10-inch tart pan with the rolled dough. Weigh down the pastry using pie weights or dried beans to prevent the crust from rising. Bake 20 minutes or until just lightly browned. Remove from oven and remove weights. (Discard beans or save them for your next pie.)

3 Decrease oven temperature to 350°F.

4 In a large bowl, beat the eggs lightly. Add the milk, garlic, salt, oregano, and Tabasco; beat until combined.

5 Sprinkle the feta cheese into the bottom of the tart shell. Pour in the egg mixture. Arrange the tomato slices on top, overlapping slices to form a single layer.

6 Bake 1 hour or until puffy and slightly browned on top.

VARIATION Sprinkle 1/4 cup sliced black olives over the tomatoes.

TARTS AND QUICHES

I usually serve tarts and quiches to large crowds because they're easy to prepare and only require a green salad to make into a complete meal (they're also great for brunch and lunch). It's the kind of meal I feel comfortable serving both vegetarians and nonvegetarians because no one ever feels left out or deprived (unless, of course, my guests are vegans—in which case I'd make a different menu entirely).

For a buffet, I generally serve two or three different types of tart or quiche—and the best part is that you can bake them in advance and freeze until needed. Just defrost, then reheat about 20 minutes at 350°F (although, honestly, I do prefer them fresh from the oven). A large salad and some bread complete the buffet table.

When baking a tart or quiche it's essential that the crust be intact with no little cracks or holes; otherwise the custard will seep through the cracks and into the crust, making it very soggy.

RISOTTO ALLA MILANESE

MAKES 2 2/3 CUPS • SERVES 3 TO 4

This is the classic way of preparing risotto. It is important that you find Arborio rice (a medium-grain white rice) as long-grain rice will not become creamy enough. In addition to the sun-dried tomato variation, which can be made year-round, you can sauté fresh, seasonal additions such as chopped asparagus, tomatoes and basil, mushrooms, or squash and stir into the risotto with the last addition of broth. When adding fresh vegetables, substitute additional broth or white wine for the Marsala so the vegetable flavors come through more clearly.

2 1/2 cups vegetable broth (homemade, page 158, or store-bought)
1 cup water
1/3 cup Marsala
Pinch saffron (optional)
2 tablespoons butter or margarine
1/3 cup finely chopped onion
1 cup Arborio rice
1/2 cup grated Parmesan cheese (optional)

1 In a 2-quart saucepan, heat the broth, water, Marsala, and saffron, if desired, until simmering. Lower the heat so the liquids just stay warm.

2 Meanwhile, melt the butter or margarine in a 3-quart saucepan, over medium heat. Add the onion; cook, stirring, until golden, about 10 minutes. Add the rice; cook, stirring, until rice is coated with butter or margarine.

3 Add the broth to the rice mixture, 1/4 cup at a time, stirring constantly, until the rice has absorbed the liquid. (You should make the next addition of liquid when you can draw a clear path on the bottom of the pot as you scrape through the rice with a wooden spoon. This will happen rather quickly at first and will take longer as you near the end of the cooking time.)

4 Stir in the Parmesan cheese, if desired, and serve.

VEGAN VARIATION Omit the cheese and stir in 1/2 cup chopped oil-marinated sun-dried tomatoes when you add the last 1/4 cup broth.

LO LACTO-OVO **L** LACTO **V** VEGAN **✳** VEGAN VARIATION **M** MAKE-AHEAD

R ISOTTO

Risotto, a very popular, creamy Italian rice dish, is made with a special medium-short-grain rice called Arborio. The starchiness of the rice gives risotto its creamy texture, which is developed by the constant stirring. Unfortunately, you can't substitute regular long-grain rice. Look for Arborio rice in your local gourmet or Italian specialty stores. Although risotto can be served as a side dish, it is more common to serve it as an entrée. A crusty bread and crispy salad will make this a meal to remember.

SHEPHERD'S PIE

MAKES 6 CUPS • SERVES 4

The 2 cups of mashed potatoes—which can be homemade or reconstituted from a package—is not a large amount. If you love potatoes, you may want to increase the quantity to 3 cups; just be sure not to cover the entire top of the pie with potatoes. Leave a little space in the middle to vent the pie as it cooks.

2 tablespoons vegetable oil
3/4 cup chopped onion
1 clove garlic, minced
2 tablespoons all-purpose flour
1 1/3 cups vegetable broth (homemade, page 158, or store-bought)
1/4 teaspoon dried thyme
1/8 teaspoon salt, or to taste
1/8 teaspoon ground black pepper
2 cups cooked brown lentils (page 171)
One 10-ounce package frozen mixed vegetables
2 cups mashed potatoes (page 139 or from potato flakes)

1 Preheat the oven to 350°F. Grease a 9 x 5 x 3-inch loaf pan.

2 In a 1 1/2-quart saucepan, heat the oil over medium-high heat. Add the onion and garlic; cook, stirring, until softened, about 2 minutes. Stir in the flour until absorbed. Add the broth, thyme, salt, and pepper. Cook, stirring, until mixture comes to a boil. Stir in the lentils and mixed vegetables. Spoon into pan.

3 Place the potatoes into a pastry bag fitted with a large star tip. Pipe the potatoes around the edge of the pan, then fill in, leaving a hole in the middle to vent.

4 Bake 40 minutes or until potatoes are browned on top.

VARIATION Use any cooked vegetables you like, such as zucchini, mushrooms, or celery.

MUSHROOM STROGANOFF

MAKES 2 1/2 CUPS • SERVES 4

I use Portobello mushrooms for this dish because they are large and meaty. I slice them into strips similar to the pieces of meat used in classic beef stroganoff. I like to serve this with broad noodles, although rice is probably more traditional.

1/4 cup sour cream
1/4 cup plain yogurt
2 tablespoons snipped fresh dill
1 teaspoon Dijon mustard
1/8 teaspoon salt, or to taste
1/8 teaspoon ground black pepper
2 tablespoons butter or margarine
6 medium Portobello mushrooms, sliced into 1/4-inch-thick strips
2 tablespoons minced onion
2 tablespoons all-purpose flour
1/2 cup vegetable broth (homemade, page 158, or store-bought)

1 In a small bowl, stir together the sour cream, yogurt, dill, mustard, salt, and pepper.

2 In a large skillet, melt the butter or margarine over medium-high heat. Add the mushrooms and onion; cook, stirring, until soft, about 6 minutes.

3 Stir in the flour until absorbed. Stir in the broth to deglaze the pan. Cook, stirring, until broth boils. Stir in the sour cream mixture. Cook, stirring, until heated through, about 1 minute longer.

VARIATION Omit the dill and substitute 1/4 cup chopped fresh parsley.

ENTRÉES

SPANAKOPITA

MAKES 24 PIECES • SERVES 8 TO 14

This is a Greek specialty that will be called *your* specialty by family and friends. It's like lasagna, but the layers are separated by buttery phyllo dough instead of noodles. This also makes a wonderful appetizer—just cut it into smaller pieces. You can make this ahead and reheat for 10 to 15 minutes at 350°F; the layers will recrisp nicely.

1 tablespoon olive oil
1 1/2 cups chopped onions
2 cloves garlic, minced
2 eggs
1 1/2 cups (12 ounces) ricotta cheese
8 ounces feta cheese, crumbled
Two 10-ounce packages frozen chopped spinach, thawed and
    squeezed dry
2/3 to 3/4 cup plain, dry bread crumbs, divided
3 tablespoons snipped fresh dill
1/8 teaspoon salt, or to taste
1/8 teaspoon ground black pepper
16 sheets phyllo dough (12 x 17 inches), thawed
1/2 cup melted butter or margarine

1 Preheat the oven to 350°F.

2 In a large skillet, heat the oil over medium-high heat. Add the onions and garlic; cook, stirring, until softened, about 2 minutes.

3 In a medium bowl, beat the eggs. Beat in the ricotta and feta. Stir in the onion mixture, spinach, 2 tablespoons of the bread crumbs, the dill, salt, and pepper; set aside.

4 Remove the phyllo sheets from the package. (Reseal the package tightly so the remaining sheets won't dry out.) Place 1 sheet on a flat surface. Brush with butter or margarine and sprinkle with about 2 teaspoons of the bread crumbs.

5 Place the next phyllo sheet on top of the first, brush with more butter or margarine, and sprinkle with bread crumbs, as before. Repeat with the third through seventh sheets. Place

100 BEST VEGETARIAN RECIPES

the eighth sheet of phyllo on top of the stack, but don't brush with butter or margarine or sprinkle with crumbs.

6 Fit the stack of phyllo into a greased 9 x 13 x 2-inch pan. Spoon the spinach-cheese filling onto the phyllo and spread to the edges. On a flat surface, layer the remaining sheets of phyllo, brushing butter or margarine and sprinkling with bread crumbs between each layer, as in step 5. Place on top of the spinach filling, and tuck edges into the pan. Using a sharp knife, score the top layers of phyllo dough into 2-inch diamonds or squares.

7 Bake 1 hour 15 minutes or until phyllo is flaky and browned.

LENTIL BURGERS

MAKES 4 PATTIES • SERVES 4

Serve these on a bun, like a regular burger, or on a plate with tomato sauce.

1 tablespoon vegetable oil, plus additional oil for frying
1 cup chopped white mushrooms
1/2 cup chopped onion
1 cup cooked brown lentils (page 171)
1 tablespoon soy sauce
1/2 cup cooked barley (page 169)
1/3 cup finely chopped walnuts
2 tablespoons plain, dry bread crumbs
1/4 teaspoon ground black pepper

1 In a medium skillet, heat 1 tablespoon of the oil over medium-high heat. Add the mushrooms and onion; cook, stirring, until softened, about 3 minutes. Reduce heat to low; add the lentils and soy sauce. Mash with fork; continue cooking until a film forms on the pan.

2 Remove from heat. Stir in the barley, walnuts, bread crumbs, and pepper. Let cool.

3 Form mixture into 4 patties. Chill at least 1 hour.

4 Pour 1/4 inch oil into a large skillet. Heat over medium-high heat until the oil bubbles when a few bread crumbs are dropped in. Cook patties until browned and crusty on bottom; turn and cook on second side.

VARIATION Use chopped pecans instead of walnuts.

NOODLES WITH PEANUT SAUCE

MAKES 4 1/2 CUPS • SERVES 4 TO 6

I get my noodles for this dish in my local Chinatown, where the lo mein noodles are sold fresh, not dried. These noodles are square egg noodles, similar in diameter to spaghetti. If you don't have access to fresh lo mein noodles, you can use 8 ounces of thin spaghetti. Although you can make this dish ahead, the noodles soak up the sauce and you may want to stir in some water before serving. Or just make the noodles and store them in a plastic bag in the refrigerator, prepare the sauce, then combine them and add the scallions just before serving.

12 ounces lo mein noodles
1/4 cup smooth peanut butter
3 tablespoons soy sauce
1 tablespoon mirin (rice wine) or dry sherry
2 teaspoons apple cider vinegar
2 teaspoons sugar
1 teaspoon chili oil
1/2 small clove garlic
1/3 cup sliced scallions

1 Cook the noodles according to package directions. Drain and rinse under cold water until cool.

2 While the noodles are cooking, place the peanut butter, soy sauce, mirin, vinegar, sugar, chili oil, and garlic in a blender or food processor. Cover and process until thoroughly combined.

3 Toss noodles with peanut sauce and scallions.

VARIATION Toss 1 cup blanched bean sprouts or julienned cucumber with the noodles and sauce.

INDONESIAN VEGETABLE STEW

MAKES 5 CUPS • SERVES 3 TO 4

I like to serve this vegetable dish over jasmine rice, using the tofu suggested in the variation. It makes the meal seem more complete. Slicing the vegetables into very thin strips (julienne) helps them cook quickly and evenly, and makes a lovely presentation.

3 tablespoons white vinegar

3 shallots, quartered

1 tablespoon minced fresh gingerroot

4 cloves garlic

2 teaspoons paprika

2 teaspoons sugar

1 1/2 teaspoons ground turmeric

1/2 teaspoon salt, or to taste

3 tablespoons vegetable oil

2 cups julienned carrots

1 1/2 cups julienned green bell peppers

1 seeded, slivered jalapeño

1 cup julienned celery

3 cups whole green beans, trimmed (about 3/4 pound)

3/4 cup unsweetened coconut milk (homemade, page 163, or store-bought)

2 tablespoons smooth peanut butter

1 Place the vinegar, shallots, ginger, garlic, paprika, sugar, turmeric, and salt into a blender. Cover and puree until a paste forms.

2 In a wok or large skillet, heat the oil over high heat. Add the spice paste; cook, stirring, 30 seconds. Add the carrots, peppers, jalapeño, celery, and green beans. Cook, stirring, 3 minutes or until vegetables are tender-crisp.

3 Add the coconut milk and peanut butter to the blender. Cover and blend until combined. Add the mixture to the skillet and deglaze the bottom of the pan. Cook, covered, 3 to 5 minutes or until the vegetables reach desired consistency.

4 Remove the cover and cook, stirring, until vegetables are tender and sauce is thickened.

VARIATION Stir julienned baked tofu into the vegetables just after you uncover the skillet.

ENTRÉES

ALMOND DING VEGETABLES

MAKES 5 CUPS • SERVES 4

When I was a kid we'd go to Ding Ho Palace for Chinese food and we frequently ordered Chicken Almond Ding. This is a lovely meatless version of that dish. You can toast the almonds, cut up the vegetables, and make the sauce in advance, but you must cook this just before serving. For a heartier dish, stir in seitan or sliced baked tofu when you add the water chestnuts. Serve with brown or white rice.

1/2 cup coarsely chopped almonds
1/4 cup water
3 tablespoons mirin (rice wine) or dry sherry
1 tablespoon soy sauce
1 tablespoon cornstarch
1/2 teaspoon sugar
2 tablespoons vegetable oil
4 cups diced celery
1 cup coarsely chopped onion
3 cloves garlic, minced
One 8-ounce can whole water chestnuts, drained and quartered
One 8-ounce can bamboo shoots, drained and diced

1 Toast almonds in a 350°F oven for 10 minutes; set aside.

2 In a small bowl, stir together the water, mirin, soy sauce, cornstarch, and sugar; set aside.

3 In a wok or large skillet, heat the oil over high heat. Add the celery, onions, and garlic; cook, stirring, until tender-crisp, about 3 minutes. Add the water chestnuts and bamboo shoots; cook, stirring, until heated through.

4 Add the cornstarch mixture; cook, stirring, until thickened, 1 to 2 minutes. Stir in the toasted almonds. Serve right away.

VARIATION Add 1 cup chopped snow peas when you add the celery.

LO LACTO-OVO   L LACTO   V VEGAN   ✷ VEGAN VARIATION   M MAKE-AHEAD

SUKIYAKI

MAKES 6 CUPS • SERVES 2 TO 3

I prepare this flavorful dish of vegetables with tofu and noodles at least once a month. I like using the firm silken tofu, but any tofu will do. If you can't find cellophane noodles—also called "bean threads"—you can use very thin rice noodles or just leave out the noodles entirely. Dark soy sauce can be found in Asian grocery stores and sometimes in the international section of your supermarket. If you can't find it, use La Choy™.

2 ounces cellophane noodles
Boiling water for soaking noodles and mushrooms
6 dried shiitake mushrooms
1/4 cup vegetable broth (homemade, page 158, or store-bought)
3 tablespoons sake, mirin (rice wine), or sherry
3 tablespoons dark soy sauce
1 1/2 tablespoons sugar
1 tablespoon vegetable oil
1 cup thinly sliced onion
2 scallions, sliced into 2-inch pieces
1 bunch fresh watercress (6 to 8 ounces), thoroughly rinsed
1 cup mung bean sprouts
1/2 cup thinly sliced carrot
8 ounces tofu, cubed

1 In a medium bowl, soak noodles in enough boiling water to cover for 15 minutes or until softened; drain and set aside.

2 In a small bowl, soak the mushrooms in enough boiling water to cover for 5 minutes. Discard the tough stems, halve the mushrooms, and set aside; reserve soaking liquid.

3 In a small bowl, stir together the broth, sake, soy sauce, sugar, and reserved mushroom liquid; set aside.

4 In a large skillet, heat the oil over high heat. Add the onions and scallions; cook, stirring, 30 seconds. Push to one side of the skillet. Add the remaining vegetables, tofu, mushrooms, and noodles, placing each in a separate section of the skillet. Pour the soy mixture into the skillet. Cover and cook on high 5 minutes or until vegetables are tender-crisp.

VARIATION Vary your vegetables—you can use bok choy, spinach, or bamboo shoots instead of, or in addition to, the watercress.

TEMPURA

MAKES 7 TO 8 CUPS • SERVES 4 TO 6

The recipe for crispy tempura is cold batter and hot oil. The batter should be thin and slightly lumpy. Good vegetable choices for tempura are thinly sliced winter squash, sweet potatoes, carrots, summer squash, green beans, bell peppers, eggplant, onions, and broccoli.

3/4 cup all-purpose flour, plus additional flour for dusting
2 tablespoons cornstarch
1 egg yolk
1 cup ice water
Oil for deep-frying
4 cups cut-up vegetables of your choice
1 recipe Asian Dipping Sauce (page 34)

1 Stir together the 3/4 cup flour and cornstarch; set aside.

2 In a medium bowl, lightly beat the egg yolk. Stir in the water until just combined. Add the flour mixture and, using a pastry cutter in an up-and-down motion, combine the flour with the egg mixture (there should still be some lumps).

3 Dust the vegetables with flour.

4 Pour oil 3 inches deep into a 3-quart pot and heat until a small piece of tempura rises to the surface after about 10 seconds. Dip the vegetables in the batter; deep-fry until lightly crispy and the vegetables are cooked, turning once if necessary. Drain on paper towels.

5 Serve with dipping sauce.

LO LACTO-OVO   **L** LACTO   **V** VEGAN   **✳** VEGAN VARIATION   **M** MAKE-AHEAD

TEMPEH WITH SATAY SAUCE

MAKES 20 SQUARES WITH 1 CUP SAUCE • SERVES 4

You can prepare the sauce and cut up the tempeh in advance, but do the frying just before serving. I use leftover sauce (and there probably will be some) as a salad dressing or dip for grilled vegetables.

2 teaspoons vegetable oil, plus additional oil for deep-frying

2 cloves garlic, minced

2 teaspoons curry powder

1 cup unsweetened coconut milk (homemade, page 163, or store-bought)

1/4 cup smooth peanut butter

2 tablespoons firmly packed light or dark brown sugar

1 tablespoon soy sauce

Two 8-ounce packages tempeh, cut into 2-inch squares

1 In a 1-quart saucepan, heat the 2 teaspoons of oil over medium-high heat. Add the garlic; cook 10 seconds, stirring, or until softened. Add the curry powder; cook, stirring, until absorbed. Stir in the coconut milk, peanut butter, brown sugar, and soy sauce. Cook, uncovered, stirring occasionally, until thickened, about 10 minutes.

2 In a medium skillet, heat enough oil over high heat to deep-fry the tempeh. Deep-fry tempeh squares until browned. Serve with peanut sauce.

VARIATION Add 1/8 teaspoon ground red pepper (or more) to the sauce when you add the curry powder.

TOFU, TEMPEH, SEITAN, AND TEXTURED VEGETABLE PROTEIN (TVP)

TOFU is made from soymilk, which is coagulated and then pressed into cakes. Tofu comes in different consistencies: firm or soft, as well as silken, which is custard-like. It can be purchased fresh (usually sold floating in a tub of water) or packaged in plastic tubs. Silken tofu is usually sold in aseptic packages; be sure to look at the expiration dates. Tofu is fairly bland and can be added to most dishes when you want to give a dish a protein boost.

In addition to fresh tofu, many health food stores sell pressed and baked tofu. Pressed tofu is usually flavored and is firmer and chewier than fresh tofu.

TEMPEH is made from cooked fermented soybeans. Tempeh can be purchased in packages in the refrigerator case of health food stores. Be sure to check the expiration dates.

The flavor of tempeh is not everyone's cup of tea, although many people feel that frying greatly improves the flavor. The texture of fried tempeh is somewhat like french fries.

SEITAN, also called "wheat gluten," is just that, the gluten from wheat. To make seitan, wheat dough is rinsed and kneaded until all that remains is the gluten, which is then cooked. It is rather chewy and meat-like in texture. It's frequently sold packed in a diluted soy sauce, which makes seitan suitable for dishes with Asian flavors.

TEXTURED VEGETABLE PROTEIN (TVP) is made from soy flour that is pressed into granules. When rehydrated, these granules have a consistency very similar to chopped meat. TVP is nearly flavorless and will assume the flavor of the dish it is cooked in.

SZECHUAN SHREDDED VEGETABLES WITH PRESSED TOFU

MAKES 5 1/2 CUPS • SERVES 4 TO 6

I think this dish is spiced just right; however, the definition of "right" varies greatly, so use more or less of the crushed red pepper to suit your own tastes. You will find pressed tofu in health food stores in the tofu section. It may also be called "baked tofu" and comes in flavors such as Thai or Mexican. The flavors are mild so you can use any of them in this dish. Serve over white or brown rice.

1/3 cup vegetable broth (homemade, page 158, or store-bought) or water

1 tablespoon soy sauce

1 tablespoon mirin (rice wine) or sherry

1 tablespoon cornstarch

2 tablespoons vegetable oil

1 tablespoon minced fresh gingerroot

3 cloves garlic, minced

1/4 teaspoon crushed red pepper

3 cups julienned carrots

2 cups julienned celery

1 cup julienned snow peas

1/2 cup julienned scallions

2 cups julienned pressed tofu

1 teaspoon sesame oil

1 In a small bowl, stir together the broth, soy sauce, mirin, and cornstarch; set aside.

2 In a wok or large skillet, heat the oil over high heat. Add the gingerroot, garlic, and red pepper; cook, stirring, 10 seconds.

3 Add the carrots, celery, snow peas, and scallions; cook, stirring, until softened, about 4 minutes. Add the tofu; cook, stirring, until heated through, about 2 minutes.

4 Add the soy mixture to the wok; cook, stirring, until sauce is thickened, about 1 minute longer. Stir in the sesame oil.

VARIATION Use julienned red or green bell peppers or bok choy instead of—or in addition to—the snow peas.

LO LACTO-OVO   **L** LACTO   **V** VEGAN   ✳ VEGAN VARIATION   **M** MAKE-AHEAD

ETHIOPIAN VEGETABLE STEW *(ATAKILT ACILCH'A)*

MAKES 6 CUPS • SERVES 4

I usually like my vegetables tender-crisp; however, the long cooking time gives the vegetables in this dish time to develop a very sweet flavor. Ethiopian dishes are usually served on a large spongy crepe called *injera*, and the crepe is also used for picking up the food. Feel free to use forks and plates and serve the stew with warm pita bread instead.

3 tablespoons vegetable oil
4 cups coarsely chopped cabbage
3 cups chopped onions
3 cloves garlic, minced
1 teaspoon turmeric
2 cups water
2 tablespoons tomato paste
3 cups carrot chunks (1 1/2- to 2-inch pieces)
3 cups whole or halved green beans (about 3/4 pound)
1 1/2 cups potato chunks (Red Bliss or other boiling potatoes)
1/2 teaspoon salt, or to taste
1/4 teaspoon ground black pepper

1 In a 6-quart pot, heat the oil over medium-high heat. Add the cabbage, onions, and garlic. Cook, stirring, until wilted, about 4 minutes. Stir in the turmeric until absorbed.

2 Add the water and tomato paste; stir until combined. Add the carrots and green beans. Bring to a boil. Reduce heat and simmer, covered, 1 1/4 hours. Add the potatoes, salt, and pepper; simmer, covered, 25 to 30 minutes longer. Add 1/4 cup additional water, if necessary.

VARIATION You can vary the vegetables to your taste. Use green peas, turnips, squash (add the squash when you add the potatoes), or any other veggies that you like.

100 BEST VEGETARIAN RECIPES

LO LACTO-OVO **L** LACTO **V** VEGAN ✳ VEGAN VARIATION **M** MAKE-AHEAD

SIDE DISHES

SIDE DISHES

What makes a side dish a side dish and not an entrée? In truth, any side dish can be a main dish, and vice versa; it just depends on what you choose to eat for a meal. I chose to resolve this question using the following criteria:

• Recipes containing primarily one vegetable became side dishes.

• Recipes that yield small portions became side dishes.

• Recipes that need "support" to be entrées (such as polenta, which requires a sauce or vegetable) became side dishes.

Here are some suggestions to help make side dishes into entrées:

• Serve a starch with a vegetable or two.

• Serve a vegetable or starch with an appetizer.

• Combine a grain dish with a bean dish.

• Double the recipe.

General cooking instructions and descriptions for grilled vegetables, grains, and beans are given in the Basic Recipes and Techniques chapter (pages 157–171).

ASPARAGUS WITH WALNUTS AND BROWNED BUTTER

MAKES 2 1/2 CUPS • SERVES 4 TO 6

Spring is the best time for asparagus (in the old days, spring was the *only* time for asparagus). Whether you use thick or thin stalks is merely a taste preference. You can also substitute any vegetable you would steam, such as green beans, cauliflower, or carrots. Be sure to stir the butter as it cooks; remove it from the heat as soon as it's lightly browned to prevent burning.

1/2 cup chopped walnuts
1 pound asparagus
2 tablespoons butter or margarine
1/2 teaspoon grated lemon zest

1 Preheat the oven to 350°F. On a baking sheet, bake the walnuts 15 minutes; set aside.

2 Prepare asparagus by holding the middle of the stalk in one hand and the bottom in the other. Bend the stalk; it will snap where the tender part starts. Discard woody ends. Steam to desired doneness; place on serving platter.

3 In a small skillet, melt the butter over medium heat; cook, stirring, until butter browns and smells nutty. Stir in the toasted walnuts and lemon zest. Pour over asparagus.

VARIATION Substitute orange zest for the lemon.

SAUTÉED EGGPLANT WITH TOMATOES, CAPERS, AND GARLIC

MAKES 3 1/2 CUPS • SERVES 4 TO 6

This is quite tangy and can even be used as a pasta sauce. If you prefer, you can peel the eggplant before cubing it.

2 tablespoons olive oil
4 cups cubed eggplant (unpeeled)
3 cloves garlic, minced
2 cups tomato wedges
1/4 cup chopped fresh parsley
1 tablespoon fresh lemon juice
1 tablespoon chopped capers
1/8 teaspoon salt, or to taste
1/8 teaspoon ground red pepper

1 In a large skillet, heat the oil over medium-high heat. Add the eggplant and garlic; cook, stirring, until slightly softened, about 3 minutes.

2 Add the tomatoes, parsley, lemon juice, capers, salt, and red pepper. Cook, stirring, until the tomatoes have softened, about 3 minutes.

VARIATION Substitute dry vermouth for the lemon juice.

SZECHUAN BROCCOLI

MAKES 9 CUPS • SERVES 6 TO 8

This recipe can be served as an entrée over rice or noodles for 3 to 4 people. Hoisin sauce is a pungent, slightly sweet thick sauce that can be found in the international section of your supermarket.

3 tablespoons water
2 tablespoons mirin (rice wine) or dry sherry
2 teaspoons soy sauce
1 tablespoon hoisin sauce
1 teaspoon cornstarch
3 tablespoons vegetable oil
1 tablespoon minced fresh gingerroot

3 cloves garlic, minced
1/4 teaspoon crushed red pepper (optional)
2 large bunches broccoli, cut into florets
1 teaspoon sesame oil

1 In a medium bowl, stir together the water, mirin, soy sauce, hoisin sauce, and cornstarch; set aside.

2 In a wok or large skillet, heat the vegetable oil over high heat. Add the gingerroot, garlic, and red pepper, if desired; cook, stirring, 30 seconds. Add the broccoli; cook, stirring, until tender-crisp, about 5 minutes.

3 Add the sauce; cook, stirring, until broccoli is coated, about 1 minute. Add the sesame oil.

VARIATION Add 1 cup sliced red or green bell peppers when you add the gingerroot and garlic.

SAUTÉED MUSHROOMS WITH WATER CHESTNUTS

MAKES 1 3/4 CUPS • SERVES 4

A lovely combination of chewy (mushrooms) and crunchy (water chestnuts), this goes well with simple stews and can even be tossed with cooked rice or any grain to jazz things up.

1 tablespoon vegetable oil
1/2 cup sliced onion
3 cups sliced white mushrooms
1/2 cup chopped canned water chestnuts
2 teaspoons soy sauce

1 In a large skillet, heat the oil over medium-high heat. Add the onion; cook, stirring, until softened, about 2 minutes. Add the mushrooms; cook, stirring, until softened, about 3 minutes.

2 Add the water chestnuts and soy sauce; cook, stirring, until any liquid has evaporated.

VARIATION Substitute 1 cup of shiitake mushrooms for 1 cup of the white mushrooms.

JALAPEÑO CARROTS

MAKES 2 1/4 CUPS • SERVES 3 TO 4

These are really not as spicy as you would imagine. You can substitute baby carrots for the julienned carrots. You can also omit the jalapeños for a simple carrot dish.

1 1/2 tablespoons butter or margarine
3 cups julienned carrots
3 tablespoons seeded, slivered jalapeños
1 1/2 tablespoons sugar
1 tablespoon water
1 teaspoon fresh lime juice
1/8 teaspoon salt, or to taste

1 In a large skillet, melt the butter or margarine over medium-high heat. Add the carrots and jalapeños; cook, stirring, until tender-crisp, about 3 minutes.

2 Add the sugar, water, lime juice, and salt. Cook, stirring, until carrots are glazed and liquid has evaporated, about 5 minutes.

VARIATION Jalapeño Jicama: Substitute julienned jicama for the carrots.

CREOLE CORN AND OKRA

MAKES 3 1/2 CUPS • SERVES 4 TO 6

If you are not fond of okra, or if it isn't available, just use the corn by itself. You can make a sort of Creole succotash by adding frozen baby or Fordhook lima beans.

1 tablespoon vegetable oil
1/2 cup chopped onion
1/2 cup chopped green bell pepper
1/2 cup chopped celery
1 1/2 cups whole okra, caps sliced off
One 11-ounce can corn kernels, undrained
One 8-ounce can tomato sauce
1/4 teaspoon salt, or to taste
1/8 teaspoon ground red pepper, or to taste

1 In a 1 1/2-quart saucepan, heat the oil over medium-high heat. Add the onion, bell pepper, and celery; cook, stirring, until tender-crisp, about 3 minutes. Add the okra; cook, stirring, until okra turns brighter green, about 2 minutes.

2 Add the corn, tomato sauce, salt, and red pepper. Bring to a boil; reduce heat and simmer, covered, 10 to 15 minutes or until the okra is tender.

VARIATION Add 1 teaspoon chili powder before adding the tomato sauce.

CAULIFLOWER POLONAISE

MAKES 4 CUPS • SERVES 4 TO 6

"Vegetables polonaise" are steamed vegetables topped with bread crumbs browned in butter. Traditionally, polonaise contains chopped egg (as in the variation), but I find it even more delicious without it. It's especially good on cauliflower because the crispy crumbs contrast the soft cauliflower texture and the brown topping contrasts with the white of the cauliflower, as well.

4 cups cauliflower florets
2 tablespoons butter or margarine
1/3 cup dry, unflavored bread crumbs
1/8 teaspoon salt, or to taste
1/8 teaspoon ground black pepper

1 Cook the cauliflower in boiling water until just tender, or to desired doneness, about 5 minutes; drain.

2 In a large skillet, melt the butter or margarine over medium-high heat. Stir in the bread crumbs; cook, stirring, until lightly browned. Stir in the salt and pepper.

3 Add the drained cauliflower; cook, stirring, until heated through.

VARIATION Add a finely chopped hard-cooked egg when you add the cauliflower.

GARLIC GREEN BEANS
MAKES 2 1/2 CUPS • SERVES 3 TO 4

I found these surprisingly mild, considering how much garlic is in the recipe. This is another recipe where you can substitute different vegetables for the green beans. Try zucchini or yellow squash, asparagus, or broccoli.

1 tablespoon olive oil
4 cups whole green beans, ends trimmed (about 3/4 pound)
1 tablespoon slivered garlic
2 teaspoons fresh lemon juice
1 tablespoon water
1/8 teaspoon salt, or to taste

In a large skillet, heat the oil over high heat. Add the green beans and garlic; cook, stirring, 1 minute. Add the lemon juice, water, and salt. Cook, stirring, until liquid evaporates and beans reach desired doneness, about 4 minutes.

VARIATION Orange-Glazed Garlic Green Beans: Add 2 teaspoons orange juice concentrate when you add the lemon juice.

COLLARDS SOUTHERN-SYLE
MAKES 2 3/4 CUPS • SERVES 3 TO 4

This is a very basic way to prepare collards; it's really good and simple to cook. You can use this recipe for any kind of greens: kale, Swiss chard, mustard greens, or any combination you prefer.

1 tablespoon olive oil
1 cup chopped onion
6 cups chopped collards
1/2 cup vegetable broth (homemade, page 158, or store-bought)

In a large skillet, heat the oil over high heat. Add the onion; cook, stirring, until transparent, about 2 minutes. Add the collards; cook, stirring, until the collards are wilted, about 2 minutes. Add the broth; simmer, covered, 15 minutes.

LIME-SAUTÉED JICAMA WITH GRAPES

V

MAKES 3 1/4 CUPS • SERVES 4 TO 6

Grapes in a savory dish? Yes! You'll be surprised at how the light sweetness of the grapes works with the other tart and mild flavors. I used red seedless grapes because they contrast nicely with the white jicama and green cilantro, but you can use green grapes, if you prefer.

1 tablespoon butter or margarine
3 cups diced jicama (1/2-inch pieces)
1/2 cup water
1 tablespoon fresh lime juice
3/4 cup halved seedless or pitted grapes
2 tablespoons chopped fresh cilantro
1/2 teaspoon grated lime zest
1/8 teaspoon salt, or to taste

In a large skillet, melt the butter or margarine over medium-high heat. Add the jicama; cook, stirring, until tender-crisp, about 4 minutes. Add the water and lime juice; cook, stirring, until liquid evaporates. Add the grapes, cilantro, lime zest, and salt; cook, stirring, until grapes are heated through.

VARIATION Substitute lemon juice and zest for the lime.

MINTED PEAS

MAKES 2 CUPS • SERVES 4

You can use dried mint (about 1 teaspoon), but try to find fresh because it really is better. You can also substitute frozen peas for the fresh, if fresh are not available.

1 tablespoon butter or margarine
1/4 cup sliced leeks (white and light green parts only), rinsed
2 cups shelled peas
3 tablespoons water
3 tablespoons chopped fresh mint
1/8 teaspoon salt, or to taste

1 In a 1 1/2-quart saucepan, melt the butter or margarine over medium-high heat. Add the leeks; cook, stirring, until softened, about 30 seconds.

2 Add the peas and water. Cover and cook, 10 minutes or until peas are tender. Add the mint and salt; cook, stirring, until any liquid has evaporated.

VARIATIONS Dilled Peas: Substitute dill for the mint. Pureed Peas: Omit the mint, place cooked peas into a food processor, cover, and puree, adding a little water if necessary.

CREAMED SPINACH

MAKES 1 3/4 CUPS • SERVES 3 TO 4

I must confess that I'm a great fan of Seabrook Farms frozen creamed spinach, but making it yourself is even better. The fresh spinach adds a noticeable bright flavor.

2 tablespoons butter or margarine
1 small clove garlic, minced
2 tablespoons all-purpose flour
2/3 cup vegetable broth (homemade, page 158, or store-bought)
2 tablespoons half-and-half
2 cups tightly packed chopped spinach (about 10 ounces before trimming)
1/8 teaspoon salt, or to taste

1 In a 1 1/2-quart saucepan, melt the butter or margarine over medium-high heat. Add the garlic; cook, stirring 10 seconds. Stir in the flour until absorbed.

2 Add the broth and half-and-half; cook, stirring with a whisk, until no lumps remain. Add the spinach and salt. Cook, stirring frequently, until spinach is cooked through, 3 to 5 minutes.

VEGAN VARIATION Substitute additional broth for the half-and-half.

PERFECT MASHED POTATOES

MAKES 2 1/2 CUPS • SERVES 4

There is nothing as wonderful as mashed potatoes when you're in need of a soothing food. Add as much of the milk as needed to make mashed potatoes that fit your idea of perfect. Just to gild the lily, you can add a 3-ounce package of cream cheese plus 2 tablespoons dried chives to the potatoes after you've mashed them; stir until the cream cheese melts.

3 cups peeled, cubed all-purpose potatoes (3/4 pound)
1/4 cup warm milk
1 tablespoon butter or margarine
1/4 teaspoon salt, or to taste
Ground black pepper to taste (optional)

1 In a 2-quart saucepan, bring the potatoes to a boil in enough water to cover them by 1 inch. Reduce heat to medium-high and cook 15 to 20 minutes or until potatoes are fork-tender. Drain immediately.

2 Return potatoes to the pot and add the remaining ingredients. For smooth mashed potatoes, mash with an electric beater until desired consistency (but don't overmix or the potatoes will become gooey). For lumpy potatoes, mash with a fork or potato masher to desired consistency.

VARIATION Stir in chopped fresh garlic, dill, chives, or scallions.

VEGAN VARIATION Substitute vegetable broth for the milk. You can also add some crushed fresh garlic.

POTATOES AU GRATIN

MAKES ONE 8-INCH SQUARE • SERVES 8 TO 12

This is real comfort food, especially on a cold winter's eve. Don't skip the blanching (step 2) or the potatoes will never soften enough when baked.

6 cups peeled, sliced baking potatoes (1/4-inch-thick pieces)
2 tablespoons butter or margarine
2 tablespoons all-purpose flour
1 3/4 cups milk
1 1/4 cups shredded Swiss cheese, divided
3 tablespoons grated Parmesan cheese, divided
1 clove garlic, minced
1/2 teaspoon salt, or to taste
1/8 teaspoon ground black pepper
1/4 teaspoon paprika

1 Preheat the oven to 350°F. Grease an 8-inch square baking dish.

2 Cook the potatoes in boiling water 5 to 7 minutes or until tender; drain.

3 In a 1-quart saucepan, melt the butter or margarine over medium-high heat. Stir in the flour until absorbed. Using a whisk, stir in the milk. Cook, stirring, until mixture comes to a boil. Remove from heat; stir in 3/4 cup of the Swiss cheese, 2 tablespoons of the grated Parmesan, the garlic, salt, and pepper.

4 Arrange half of the potatoes in the baking pan. Pour 1/2 of the sauce over the potatoes. Repeat with remaining potatoes and sauce. Sprinkle top with remaining 1/2 cup Swiss and 1 tablespoon Parmesan cheese; sprinkle lightly with paprika.

5 Bake 30 to 40 minutes or until browned on top. Let stand 10 minutes before serving.

VARIATION Use Cheddar cheese instead of the Swiss cheese.

PESTO VEGETABLES

MAKES 3 1/2 CUPS • SERVES 6

I always keep some homemade pesto in my freezer to jazz up simple recipes. If you didn't make pesto this summer, you can always buy some at the supermarket.

1 tablespoon olive oil
1 cup julienned carrots
2 cups diced zucchini
1 cup diced yellow squash
3 tablespoons pesto
2 tablespoons grated Parmesan cheese (optional)

In a large skillet, heat the olive oil over medium-high heat. Add the carrots and sauté 1 minute. Add the zucchini and yellow squash; cook, stirring, until softened, about 3 minutes. Add the pesto; add the Parmesan cheese, if desired.

VEGAN VARIATION Omit the Parmesan cheese and make sure your pesto sauce doesn't contain cheese.

PUREED WINTER SQUASH WITH PEARS

MAKES 1 2/3 CUPS • SERVES 3 TO 4

It's very important to use ripe and juicy pears so the pear flavor is maximized. This dish is slightly but not overly sweet; you may choose to add a bit more brown sugar to your own taste.

2 cups peeled, diced calabaza or butternut squash
2 cups peeled, diced ripe pears
2 tablespoons white wine or water
1 tablespoon firmly packed light or dark brown sugar
1/2 teaspoon ground cinnamon
1 teaspoon fresh lemon juice

1 Place the squash, pears, wine, brown sugar, and cinnamon in a 1 1/2-quart saucepan. Bring to a boil over medium heat. Reduce heat and simmer, 30 minutes, uncovered, until the squash is soft.

2 Place the squash, pears, and any liquid, along with the lemon juice, in a blender or food processor. Cover and process until smooth.

VARIATION Add 1/8 to 1/4 teaspoon ground nutmeg when you add the cinnamon.

BASIL-STUFFED BAKED TOMATOES

MAKES 4 HALVES • SERVES 4

Stuffed tomatoes are great side dishes for any meal. You can make many variations on this recipe: try stirring in different herbs, or adding chopped celery and/or bell peppers when you add the onion.

2 ripe medium tomatoes
1 tablespoon olive oil
1/4 cup finely chopped onion
1 clove garlic, minced
1/2 cup dry, unflavored bread crumbs
3 tablespoons chopped fresh basil, or 2 teaspoons dried basil
1/8 teaspoon salt, or to taste
1/8 teaspoon ground black pepper

1 Preheat the oven to 350°F.

2 Cut the tomatoes in half. Scoop out the center tomato pulp and chop; set aside.

3 In a medium skillet, heat the oil over medium-high heat. Add the onion and garlic; cook, stirring, until onion is softened, about 2 minutes. Add the chopped tomato pulp; cook, stirring, until softened, about 2 minutes. Stir in the bread crumbs, basil, salt, and pepper.

4 Fill each tomato half with 1/4 of the bread crumb mixture.

5 Bake 15 minutes or until heated through.

VARIATION Use flavored bread crumbs instead of plain. Add 2 tablespoons grated Parmesan cheese, if desired.

SIDE DISHES

BARLEY WITH MUSHROOMS

MAKES 3 1/4 CUPS • SERVES 4 TO 6

Dress up this everyday favorite by substituting wild mushrooms for the white, or adding chopped dill and/or parsley to the dish.

1 1/2 tablespoons vegetable oil
1/2 cup chopped onion
1/2 cup chopped bell pepper
1 1/2 cups sliced white mushrooms
1 2/3 cups water
1/2 teaspoon salt, or to taste
1/4 teaspoon ground black pepper
3/4 cup pearl barley

1 In a 2-quart saucepan, heat the oil over medium-high heat. Add the onion and bell pepper; cook, stirring, until softened, about 3 minutes. Add the mushrooms; cook, stirring, until softened, about 3 minutes.

2 Add the water, salt, and pepper; bring to a boil. Stir in the barley; return to a boil. Reduce heat and simmer, covered, 40 minutes or until liquid is absorbed.

VARIATION Substitute broth for the water and adjust salt accordingly.

CURRIED MILLET

MAKES 3 1/3 CUPS • SERVES 4 TO 6

This curry has a pretty good kick to it. If you prefer a milder curry, use only a pinch of the ground red pepper or eliminate it altogether.

1 1/2 tablespoons vegetable oil
3/4 cup millet, rinsed
3/4 cup chopped onion
2 cloves garlic, minced
1 tablespoon curry powder
1/2 teaspoon ground cumin
1/2 teaspoon ground turmeric
1/4 teaspoon ground red pepper, or to taste
1 1/2 cups water
1/2 teaspoon salt, or to taste

1 In a 1 1/2-quart saucepan, heat the oil over medium-high heat. Add the millet; cook, stirring, until the millet crackles, about 2 minutes.

2 Add the onion and garlic; cook, stirring, until softened, about 2 minutes. Stir in the curry powder, cumin, turmeric, and red pepper until absorbed.

3 Add the water and salt. Reduce heat and simmer, covered, 20 to 25 minutes or until liquid is absorbed. Remove from heat and fluff with a fork. Let stand 5 minutes before serving.

VARIATION Add 1/2 cup frozen peas 5 minutes before the millet has finished cooking. You can also stir in some chopped cashews and dark raisins.

SIDE DISHES

QUINOA WITH MIXED VEGETABLES

MAKES 3 CUPS • SERVES 4 TO 6

I wrote this recipe to be cooked with barley, but when I went to the pantry I was all out, so I used quinoa instead. Just proof that happy accidents do occur!

1/2 cup quinoa
1 tablespoon vegetable oil
1 cup chopped white mushrooms
3/4 cup chopped carrots
1/2 cup chopped onion
1/2 cup chopped bell pepper
1/2 cup chopped celery
3/4 cup vegetable broth (homemade page 158 or store-bought)
1/2 cup corn kernels (fresh; canned, drained; or frozen)
1/8 teaspoon ground black pepper

1 Place the quinoa in a large bowl; fill bowl with cool water and then drain into a strainer. Repeat 4 more times or until the water no longer looks soapy.

2 In a 2-quart saucepan, heat the oil over medium-high heat. Add the mushrooms, carrots, onion, bell pepper, and celery. Cook, stirring, until vegetables are softened, and any liquid has evaporated, about 4 minutes.

3 Add the broth; bring to a boil. Stir in the quinoa; return to a boil. Reduce heat and simmer, covered, 15 minutes.

4 Stir in the corn; return to a simmer. Simmer, covered, 5 minutes longer or until liquids are absorbed. Remove from heat; stir in pepper. Let stand 3 minutes.

VARIATION Substitute chopped zucchini for the corn.

RICE PILAF

MAKES 4 CUPS • SERVES 6 TO 8

V
M

Pilaf is a popular way to prepare many different grains: barley, wild rice, or millet. I think it works best with grains that cook in less than an hour so the onions don't become too mushy.

1 tablespoon olive oil
1 cup chopped onion
1 clove garlic, minced
2 1/4 cups vegetable broth (homemade, page 158, or store-bought)
1 cup converted long-grain white rice
1/4 teaspoon salt, or to taste
1/8 teaspoon ground black pepper

1 In a 1 1/2-quart saucepan, heat the oil over medium-high heat. Add the onion and garlic; cook, stirring, until softened, about 2 minutes. Add the broth and bring to a boil.

2 Add the rice and return to a boil. Reduce heat and simmer, covered, 20 to 25 minutes or until liquid is absorbed. Remove from heat; stir in the salt and pepper; let stand, covered, 5 minutes.

VARIATIONS Saffron Rice: Add 1/4 teaspoon saffron threads when you add the broth.
Rice Pilau: To make a rice pilau to serve with curry, add 1/2 teaspoons coriander seeds, 1/2 teaspoon ground turmeric, 1/4 teaspoon ground cumin, and 1/4 teaspoon ground allspice to the cooked onion before adding the broth.

AUTUMN BROWN RICE

MAKES 3 CUPS • SERVES 4 TO 6

Squash and cranberries are a natural contrast between sweet and tart and the textures of the rice compliments the other ingredients as well. Play around with this. You can use any dried fruit for the cranberries—how about pine nuts (*pignoli*) instead of the walnuts?

1 1/2 cups water
2/3 cup brown rice
3/4 cup peeled, diced butternut squash
3/4 cup chopped walnuts or pecans
1/2 cup chopped dried cranberries
2 tablespoons honey
1/4 teaspoon salt, or to taste

1 In a 1 1/2-quart saucepan, bring the water to a boil over high heat. Add the rice; return to a boil. Reduce heat and simmer, covered, 35 minutes.

2 Add the squash; cover and simmer 10 minutes longer or until the water is absorbed and the squash and rice are tender.

3 Stir in the nuts, cranberries, honey, and salt. Cook until heated through.

VARIATION Use apples instead of cranberries.

LO LACTO-OVO **L** LACTO **V** VEGAN **✷** VEGAN VARIATION **M** MAKE-AHEAD

WILD RICE WITH ORZO AND THREE-COLOR PEPPERS

MAKES 3 1/4 CUPS • SERVES 4 TO 6

This started out as a rice dish, but I was concerned that cooking the peppers with the rice might result in overcooked vegetables. Fortune stepped in—I had cooked orzo left over from another dish, so that's how this one was developed.

1 tablespoon olive oil
3/4 cup chopped onion
1/2 cup chopped green bell pepper
1/2 cup chopped red bell pepper
1/2 cup chopped yellow bell pepper
1 cup cooked orzo
3/4 cup cooked wild rice
1/4 teaspoon salt, or to taste

1 In a medium skillet, heat the oil over medium-high heat. Add the onion and all three bell peppers; cook, stirring, until softened, about 4 minutes.

2 Stir in the orzo, wild rice, and salt. Cook until heated through.

VARIATION Wild and White or Brown Rice with Three-Color Peppers: Use cooked white or brown rice instead of the orzo.

LO LACTO-OVO **L** LACTO **V** VEGAN **✳** VEGAN VARIATION **M** MAKE-AHEAD

COUSCOUS WITH GOLDEN FRUIT AND VEGETABLES

MAKES 4 CUPS • SERVES 6 TO 8

This is a wonderful accompaniment to all curries, especially Curried Chickpeas and Kale (page 90).

2 teaspoons vegetable oil
1/3 cup chopped onion
1 teaspoon curry powder
1/2 teaspoon ground cinnamon
1 1/3 cups water
1/2 cup chopped carrots
3/4 cup peeled, chopped butternut squash (or buttercup or calabaza)
3/4 cup couscous
1/2 cup chopped dried apricots
1/4 cup golden raisins
1/3 cup chopped pecans
1/2 teaspoon salt, or to taste

1 In a 2-quart saucepan, heat the oil over medium-high heat. Add the onion; cook, stirring, until transparent, about 2 minutes.

2 Stir in the curry powder and cinnamon until absorbed. Add the water and bring to a boil. Add the carrots and squash; simmer, covered, 7 minutes or until vegetables are tender.

3 Add the couscous, apricots, and raisins. Cover and simmer 2 minutes. Remove from heat and let stand, covered, 3 minutes longer. Add the pecans and salt; toss to combine.

VARIATION Use chopped rutabaga (yellow turnip) instead of the squash.

SIDE DISHES

FRIJOLES

MAKES 2 1/2 CUPS • SERVES 3 TO 4

The Mexican method is to cook dried beans without presoaking them. These beans are unbelievably delicious. Use them on tostadas, in burritos, or alongside other Mexican entrées.

3 cups water
1 cup dry pinto, black, or kidney beans
1/2 cup chopped onion
1 tablespoon minced, seeded jalapeño, or to taste
3 cloves garlic, minced, divided
1 bay leaf
1/4 teaspoon salt, or to taste
1 tablespoon vegetable oil
1/2 cup peeled, seeded, and chopped tomatoes
Chopped cilantro, garnish

1 In a 2-quart saucepan, combine the water, beans, onion, jalapeño, 1 teaspoon of the garlic, and the bay leaf. Bring to a boil over medium heat. Reduce heat and simmer, covered, until beans are tender, about 1 1/2 hours. Stir in the salt and discard the bay leaf; simmer 30 minutes longer.

2 In a small skillet, heat the oil over medium-high heat. Add the tomatoes and remaining garlic. Cook, stirring, until tomatoes soften, about 3 minutes.

3 Place the tomatoes and 1/4 cup of the beans in a food processor fitted with a metal blade. Cover and blend until smooth. Return mixture to the bean pot and cook, uncovered, 10 minutes longer.

VARIATION Add the tomatoes to the pot without pureeing them.

WHEAT BERRIES WITH GINGERED EGGPLANT

MAKES 1 3/4 CUPS • SERVES 3 TO 4

You could eliminate the wheat berries from this dish and have a very nice eggplant spread.

1 1/2 tablespoons vegetable oil
1 tablespoon minced fresh gingerroot
2 cloves garlic, minced
2 cups finely diced eggplant (unpeeled)
2 tablespoons mirin (rice wine) or dry sherry
1 teaspoon soy sauce
1 1/2 cups cooked wheat berries (page 167)
1 1/2 teaspoons rice vinegar
1/4 teaspoon chili oil

1 In a large skillet, heat the vegetable oil over medium-high heat. Add the gingerroot and garlic; cook, stirring, until softened, 30 seconds.

2 Add the eggplant; cook, stirring, until oil is absorbed, about 2 minutes. Add the mirin and soy sauce; cook 5 minutes or until eggplant is cooked through. Add the wheat berries; cook until heated through. Stir in the vinegar and chili oil.

VARIATION For a milder version, use sesame oil instead of chili oil.

BARBECUE BEANS

MAKES 2 1/2 CUPS • SERVES 4

When I call for pepper sauce in this recipe I'm not referring to
Tabasco sauce or any other hot sauce, but rather a thick, brown
sauce with a fruit base that usually includes tamarind (one brand
is Pickapeppa Sauce). If you don't have pepper sauce, you can
substitute steak sauce. You can use any type of cooked beans
instead of the kidney beans.

1 cup chopped tomatoes

1/2 cup water

2 tablespoons tomato paste

1 1/2 tablespoons firmly packed light or dark brown sugar

1 1/2 tablespoons white vinegar

1 tablespoon molasses

2 teaspoons pepper sauce

1/2 teaspoon anchovy-free Worcestershire sauce

2 cloves garlic, minced

1/8 teaspoon salt, or to taste

4 drops hot sauce, or to taste

2 teaspoons vegetable oil

1/2 cup chopped onion

1/2 cup finely chopped bell pepper

2 cups cooked red kidney beans (cooked from dry; or canned,
drained)

1 In a medium bowl, stir together the tomatoes, water,
tomato paste, brown sugar, vinegar, molasses, pepper sauce,
Worcestershire sauce, garlic, salt, and hot sauce; set aside.

2 In a 2-quart saucepan, heat the oil over medium-high heat.
Add the onion and bell pepper; cook, stirring, until softened,
about 3 minutes. Stir in the sauce mixture; bring to a boil.
Reduce heat and simmer 15 minutes.

3 Stir in the beans. Simmer 10 minutes longer or until heated
through.

VARIATION Barbecue Sauce: Omit the beans and use the
sauce as desired. Makes 1 1/2 cups sauce.

LENTILS IN TOMATO SAUCE

MAKES: 3 CUPS • SERVES: 3 TO 4

This highly seasoned dish tastes equally good served warm or at room temperature. If you puree the lentils, as suggested in the variation, you get a puree with some Ethiopian flavor—just add extra ground red pepper.

1 tablespoon olive oil
1/2 cup chopped onion
2 cloves garlic, minced
1/2 cup water
2 tablespoons tomato paste
1/8 teaspoon salt, or to taste
1/4 teaspoon ground red pepper
1 1/2 cups cooked lentils

1 In a 1 1/2-quart saucepan, heat the oil over medium-high heat. Add the onion and garlic; cook, stirring, until softened, about 2 minutes.

2 Add the water, tomato paste, salt, and red pepper; stir until combined. Add the lentils; cook, uncovered, 5 minutes or until heated through.

VARIATION Place the lentils in a food processor container fitted with a steel blade. Cover and process until pureed.

LO LACTO-OVO L LACTO V VEGAN ✳ VEGAN VARIATION M MAKE-AHEAD

BASIC RECIPES AND TECHNIQUES

COOKING BASICS

B ROTH

If you want to use homemade broth in your recipes, freeze a batch in 1-cup packets (plastic bags or containers) so you can pull them out of the freezer as needed. For a stronger-flavored broth, shred the vegetables before cooking them. The increased surface area of the vegetables releases more flavor in the broth. Or if you have a juicer, juice the vegetables (but not the onions, leeks, or garlic), add the juice and pulp to the pot, then cook. Strain, pressing the liquid from the pulp after the broth is cooked. For more on broth see page 14.

MIGHTY VEGETABLE BROTH

MAKES 4 CUPS • SERVES 4

This is a good all-purpose broth. By itself, you may want to add salt to taste; if you're using it in a recipe, leave it unsalted, then add salt to taste after cooking the dish. Parsley root is just that—the root of the parsley plant. It looks a lot like parsnip, and if you are lucky it will come with the flat-leaf parsley leaves still attached (that way you don't have to buy a bunch of parsley).

8 cups water
3 medium carrots (6 ounces), peeled
2 large ribs celery, with leaves (6 ounces)
2 medium parsnips (6 ounces), peeled
2 leeks, thoroughly rinsed
2 small parsley roots, including leaves, peeled
1 medium turnip (6 ounces), peeled
1 medium tomato (6 ounces)
1/2 small celeriac (celery root, knob celery; 3 ounces), peeled
2 cloves garlic

1 Place all the ingredients in a 4-quart pot. Bring to a boil over high heat. Reduce heat and simmer, covered, 1 hour. Uncover and simmer 1 hour longer.

2 Place a large, fine strainer over a large bowl. Pour the broth and vegetables into the strainer. Gently press the vegetables remaining in the strainer, until all the liquid has fallen into the bowl. Discard pressed vegetables.

VARIATION Add any vegetables you have on hand: cabbage, spinach, onion, kohlrabi, and so on.

BASIC GRILLED OR BROILED VEGETABLES

YIELD DEPENDS ON TYPE AND QUANTITY OF VEGETABLES USED

For vegetables such as eggplant, summer squash, or fennel, use the recipe below. For bell peppers (any color) omit the oil. Cut into quarters or eighths, discard pith and seeds, and cook until charred on both sides. Place in a paper bag and let cool, then remove the skin. For easier cleanup, line the (ungreased) cookie sheet with aluminum foil, then grease the foil. When making roasted peppers, roll them up in the foil and allow them to cool in the foil packet. This will create steam and make it easier to remove the skins.

Vegetables of choice, sliced into 1/2-inch-thick pieces
Olive or vegetable oil

1 Preheat the grill or broiler.

2 Lightly brush each side of the vegetable slices with oil and place on lightly greased cookie sheet.

3 Broil 4 to 6 inches from heat, 5 minutes per side or until browned or lightly charred on the outside and tender or tender-crisp on the inside.

VARIATION Barbecued Vegetables: Instead of brushing the vegetables with oil, brush them with barbecue sauce (homemade, page 155, or store-bought).

LOWER-FAT VARIATION Instead of using oil, make a mixture of 1/2 cup broth, 2 cloves garlic, minced, and 1 teaspoon olive oil.

BASIC POLENTA

MAKES 2 1/2 CUPS • SERVES 4

This Italian specialty is a filling side dish for vegetables and stews. It's very versatile and can also be served with just about any sauce you'd serve on pasta. You can also put the polenta into a loaf pan to cool, then slice and fry until golden on both sides. Fried polenta makes a great first course when topped with Eggplant with Red Peppers and Shiitake Mushrooms (page 107). If you don't have the patience to make polenta from scratch, you can also use instant polenta (available in specialty stores and some supermarkets) with good results.

2 1/2 cups water
3/4 cup polenta (yellow cornmeal)
1/2 teaspoon salt, or to taste
1 tablespoon butter or margarine (optional)

1 In a 2-quart saucepan, stir together the water, polenta, and salt until there are no lumps.

2 Bring to a boil over medium-high heat, stirring frequently. Reduce heat; simmer, stirring constantly, until the polenta leaves a clean path when you scrape the bottom of the pan (and your arms feel like they are falling off), 20 to 30 minutes.

3 Add the butter or margarine, if desired, and stir until melted.

4 Serve immediately or place in loaf pan to cool for slicing.

VARIATION Creamy Polenta: Stir in 1/2 cup half-and-half or milk when you add the butter or margarine.

FRESH TOMATO SAUCE

MAKES 4 CUPS • SERVES 6 TO 8

There's nothing gentle about the flavor of this tomato sauce. It starts with fresh tomatoes and a fairly amazing amount of garlic and ends as a wonderful sauce. You can peel and seed the tomatoes if you like, but I usually don't bother in this recipe. For a Basic Tomato Sauce using canned tomatoes, use the sauce recipe for Red, Green, and White Lasagna (page 102). You can make that sauce into marinara sauce by adding the herbs in the variation to this recipe.

1/4 cup olive oil
1/3 cup paper-thin slices garlic
8 cups tomato chunks (about 3 pounds)
1/4 cup tomato paste
1/4 teaspoon salt, or to taste
Ground black pepper to taste

1 In a 4-quart pot, heat the oil over medium-high heat. Add the garlic; cook, stirring, until softened, about 30 seconds.

2 Add the tomatoes; cook until the tomatoes give off enough liquid so that most of the pieces are submerged. Stir in the tomato paste. Bring to a boil. Reduce heat to medium and cook, uncovered, 50 minutes or until thickened. Stir in the salt and pepper.

VARIATION Marinara Sauce: Stir in 1/4 cup chopped parsley, 1 1/2 teaspoons dried oregano, 1 teaspoon dried basil, and 1/4 teaspoon dried thyme when you add the tomatoes.

EASY SALSA

MAKES 2 2/3 CUPS • SERVES 12 TO 16

Not quite as easy, but even tastier, is this: start with 2 cups finely chopped fresh tomatoes instead of the canned.

One 14 1/2-ounce can whole peeled tomatoes, undrained
One 4-ounce can chopped green chiles, undrained
1/2 cup sliced scallions (white and green parts)
1/2 cup chopped onion
1/4 cup chopped fresh cilantro
2 tablespoons fresh lime juice
2 cloves garlic, minced
1/4 teaspoon ground cumin
1/4 teaspoon sugar
1/4 teaspoon salt, or to taste
1/2 cup chopped fresh tomatoes

1 Place all the ingredients in a blender or food processor. Cover and pulse until finely chopped.

2 Let stand at least one hour for the flavors to meld.

VARIATION Omit the canned chiles and substitute 1 or 2 seeded, diced fresh jalapeños.

EASY COCONUT MILK

MAKES 1 CUP

This method is not as easy as buying canned coconut milk, but at least you don't have to crack and peel the coconut. Be sure to use unsweetened coconut (usually available in health food stores), not the sweetened stuff you find in the baking section of the supermarket.

1 1/2 cups water
1 cup unsweetened shredded coconut

1 In a 1 1/2-quart saucepan, bring the water and coconut to a boil.

2 Place the mixture in a blender. Cover and blend on high speed until finely ground (about 1 minute). Pour through a strainer lined with a double layer of cheesecloth. Lift the edges of the cheesecloth and wring out as much of the liquid as possible from the coconut.

COOKING VEGETABLES

STEAMING VEGETABLES

Steaming (cooking vegetables in a covered pot, on a rack, over—not immersed in—boiling water) is the ideal way to cook vegetables because they will retain most of their vitamin content. Some vitamins are inevitably destroyed by heat during any cooking process, but many still remain with steaming.

Steamers are available in many different styles. Some are perforated metal disks with collapsible sides; others fit into the top of pots, similar to a double boiler but with holes. Asian steamers are stackable bamboo or metal cylinders that fit into a wok, which holds the boiling water. You can also improvise a steamer by placing a round rack into a pot (with a lid) and adding enough water to boil in the bottom, but not to immerse the vegetables.

The cooking times for steaming can only be approximated, since the size and quantity of the vegetables will affect the cooking time. Furthermore, doneness is strictly a matter of taste. You will need considerably less cooking time for tender-crisp vegetables than for the same vegetables to be cooked until soft. The best test for doneness is to take a bite and see if you like the consistency.

MICROWAVING VEGETABLES

My favorite method for cooking one or two portions of vegetables in the microwave is to wet a microwave-safe paper towel, wrap the vegetables in the towel, then microwave on high for a minute or two or until the vegetables reach the desired doneness. Be careful when you remove them from the oven because the towel will be quite hot.

A more conventional method of microwaving vegetables is to use a microwave steamer (two nesting bowls, plus a top) and cook until the vegetables are al dente or to desired doneness.

GRILLING VEGETABLES

Although many recipes in this book call for grilled vegetables, in fact, I usually cook them in the broiler until slightly charred. Vegetables "grilled" in the broiler have several advantages: They are easier to turn; they can be grilled year-round; and of course the broiler is easier to start than a charcoal grill. Other options for indoor grilling are electric and stove-top, smoke-free grills. Electric grills have heating units under the grill, whereas the "minute" grills have heating units on both top and bottom, which speeds up the cooking time. Top-of-the-stove grills are made of two round pieces of metal. The bottom part fits over the burner and gets filled with water. To cook, food is placed on the nonstick top, which has slots cut into it.

If you don't have any type of grill, you can broil the vegetables as described on page 159. To add more flavor, brush the vegetables with olive oil, or melted butter or margarine, or flavor the oil with pressed garlic cloves, chili or curry powder, or various herbs.

Almost any vegetable can be grilled. Zucchini, yellow squash, eggplant, and bell peppers grill extremely well. But you can also grill root vegetables (onions, carrots, beets, jicama) and potatoes, although the potatoes tend to come out like tender-crisp carrots.

For actual outdoor grilling, cut the vegetables into chunks and string them on skewers so they are easier to turn. You can brush the kebabs with any of the same items as you would for indoor-grilled vegetables.

ROASTING VEGETABLES

Root vegetables and potatoes are especially delicious when roasted. Peel the root vegetables (and the potatoes, if you prefer them that way), then slice about 1/4 inch thick. Grease a baking pan that is large enough to hold the amount of vegetables you want to make in a single layer. Drizzle a small amount of oil (olive oil is especially good) over the vegetables in the pan and toss. If you like, you can also toss unpeeled cloves of garlic and herbs in, too. Bake in a 400°F preheated oven for about 50 minutes, stirring occasionally, or until the vegetables are browned on the edges, or to your taste.

POTATO BASICS

BOILED POTATOES

Peel or scrub as many potatoes as you intend to cook. Place the potatoes in a saucepan and fill with enough water to cover the potatoes by 1 inch. Bring to a boil over high heat. Reduce heat to medium-high and cook 15 to 20 minutes or until potatoes are fork-tender. Drain immediately. If the potatoes are very large, you can cut them in halves or quarters, or just cook them longer.

BAKED POTATOES

Scrub 4 medium baking potatoes, or as many as you want—the number doesn't affect the baking time. Bake 1 hour in a 350°F oven or until potatoes are tender when lightly squeezed. Turn off the oven and leave potatoes in it for 40 minutes.

MICROWAVED BAKED POTATOES

It's very important to pierce the potatoes before placing them in the microwave oven; otherwise steam builds up as they cook and they will explode all over the oven. Lightly sprinkle salt over an 8-ounce potato. Wrap in microwave-safe paper towel (if you are cooking more than one at a time, wrap each potato in a separate paper towel). Microwave on high, turning potato upside down halfway through the cooking time (see below). Bake until potato is tender when lightly squeezed. Let stand a few minutes before serving.

MICROWAVE TIMING FOR POTATOES

The cooking times given here are based on a 650-watt microwave oven. Times may vary depending on your microwave.

POTATO	TIME
1 potato	3 minutes
2 potatoes	6 minutes
3 potatoes	8 minutes
4 potatoes	11 minutes

GRAINS

Until the late 1980s, most Americans' idea of grains was rice, wheat, corn, and barley. The wheat was usually eaten as flour in baked goods, although an occasional bulgur or couscous dish was a possibility.

As the medical community began acknowledging that eating less meat makes for healthier living, food writers started venturing further afield to find dishes that would fill the gap.

When it came to healthy eating, vegetarians had quite a jump on the population at large. Brown rice, oats, and millet were already known commodities and "newer" grains such as quinoa and kamut were not unheard of.

WHOLE GRAINS WITH HULLS

You will see that whole grains are sometimes referred to as "berries." Both terms refer to grains that are intact, with only the outer husks removed; the bran (or hull), germ, and endosperm remain.

Because of the hulls, completely unprocessed grains require long cooking times. These grains absorb the water best when there is no salt in the cooking liquid (and that includes any broths). Since the long cooking time also turns most vegetables into mush, I prefer to cook grains separately. Practically speaking, it makes sense to cook up a batch large enough for more than one recipe, then use the remainder in any recipe calling for cooked whole grain products, regardless of whether the grain called for is exactly the one you've cooked.

The flavor and consistency of whole grains are fairly similar, and you can use them interchangeably. Switching grains can be necessary when cooking for people who are allergic to certain grains (usually wheat); by substituting another grain you can still use the recipes.

COOKING WHOLE GRAINS

1 In a 1 1/2- or 2-quart saucepan bring water to boil.

2 Add the grain.

3 Return to a boil; reduce heat and simmer, covered, for specified time (see page 169) or until water is absorbed.

4 Stir lightly to fluff (add salt to taste, if desired).

5 Let stand for specified time (see page 169).

PROCESSED GRAINS

Processed grains are those that have been pretreated in some manner before packaging, such as having the hulls removed or being cracked. Following are explanations of how various grains are processed.

BARLEY

HULLESS BARLEY Specifically grown without hull. Treat like whole unprocessed grains (see chart, next page).

PEARL BARLEY Barley with hull polished (removed by grinding).

BUCKWHEAT

KASHA Toasted buckwheat; can be whole or cracked into coarse, medium, or fine grains.

WHEAT

BULGUR WHEAT Wheat that has been hulled, then steamed and dried. Available course, medium, and fine grain.

CEREAL, FARINA Very finely cracked endosperm of wheat.

CEREAL, WHEATENA Very finely cracked wheat.

CRACKED WHEAT Whole wheat that has been broken into pieces.

COOKING PROCESSED GRAINS

1 Bring water to a boil in a 1 1/2-quart saucepan.

2 Add the grain.

3 Reduce heat; simmer, covered, for specified time or until water is absorbed.

4 Stir lightly to fluff (add salt to taste, if desired).

5 Let stand for specified time.

GRAIN BASICS

Many factors determine how your grain will cook. For these reasons, cooking times and amounts of water needed are an inexact science:

• Many factors can change cooking times for whole grains: how tightly the lid fits on the saucepan, how old the grain is, how large your burner is, etc. Therefore, peek into the pot as it nears its cooking time to make sure the water hasn't evaporated and the grain isn't sticking to the bottom of the pan.

• Taste the grain; if it seems done to you, it is. If not, continue to cook, adding more water if necessary.

• Do not add salt to the cooking water when cooking whole grains. It retards the absorption of the water and the grains will not swell properly (they will cook, but the yield will probably be smaller). Adding salt after cooking will give the grain a saltier flavor; therefore, you will need less salt than if you had added it in the beginning.

• Do not stir the grains as they cook as that will bruise the grains and they will become sticky.

GRAIN COOKING TABLE

GRAIN 1 CUP	WATER (CUPS)	COOKING TIME	STANDING TIME	YIELD (CUPS)
Couscous	1 3/4	2 min.	3 min.	2 3/4
Grits (quick)	4	5 min.	1 min.	4
Barley (pearl)	2 1/2	40 min.	4 min.	3 1/2
Bulgur and cracked wheat	2	20 min.	3 min.	3
Kamut	1 1/2	1 hr.	3 min.	2 1/2
Kasha (whole)	2	10 to 15 min.	5 min.	3
Millet*	2	20 to 30 min.	5 min.	4
Oats (whole)	2	1 hr.	7 min.	2 1/2
Quinoa**	2	15 min.	5 min.	3 1/2
Spelt	2	1 1/2 hrs.	5 min.	3
Whole grain rye	2 1/2	2 hrs. 15 min.	10 min.	3 1/2
Whole grain wheat	2 1/4	1 1/2 to 2 hrs.	5 min.	2 1/2

* Sauté millet in 1 tablespoon of oil for 1 to 2 minutes before adding water.

**Rinse well before cooking.

RICE

In addition to long-grain white rice there are medium- and short-grain rice. Shorter grains yield stickier cooked rice. Medium-grained Arborio rice is prized for the creamy result it produces in risottos (see page 112). Short-grain rice is most frequently used in Asian cooking, notably for sushi and other molded rice dishes.

Imported rice varieties such as jasmine (my favorite) and basmati have a very fragrant aroma and delicate flavor (some describe it as a popcorn flavor). In fact, they are called "aromatic" rice. American growers are also producing aromatic rices called jasmati, Texmati, and Calmati.

Brown rice has a nuttier flavor and chewier consistency than white. It comes in long and short grains. It also has a higher fiber and vitamin profile. Brown rice takes longer to cook than white, but it's worth the effort.

Instant rice is widely available in supermarkets, in both white and brown varieties. It is precooked rice that has been dehydrated. Just add it to boiling water for a few minutes.

COOKING RICE

1 Bring water to a boil in a 1 1/2-quart saucepan.

2 Add the rice.

3 Reduce heat; simmer, covered, for specified time (see below) or until water is absorbed.

4 Stir lightly to fluff (add salt to taste, if desired).

5 Let stand for specified time (see below).

RICE COOKING TABLE

RICE 1 CUP	WATER (CUPS)	COOKING TIME	STANDING TIME	YIELD (CUPS)
Basmati	2	20 min.	5 min.	3 2/3
Brown	2 1/4	45 min.	2 min.	3 1/2
Converted	2 1/2	25 min.	5 min.	3 1/2
Jasmine	2	20 min.	5 min.	3
Texmati	2	20 min.	5 min.	4
White, long-grain	2	20 min.	5 min.	3
Wild rice	2	50 min.	5 min.	3

BEANS

Beans come in a wide variety of sizes and colors. Most have an earthy or smoky flavor when cooked. Cooking beans from dry will give you a wider choice of bean than canned beans, but then you have to plan to make them in advance as they need soaking time in addition to the cooking time.

1 Rinse the beans and discard any debris.

2 For each cup of beans, add 4 cups of water and soak overnight, or until the interior of the bean is uniform in color when cut in half with a sharp knife. Or quick-soak by bringing the water and beans to a boil, reducing heat and simmering 2 minutes. Turn off heat and let stand 1 hour, or until the interior of the bean is uniform in color when cut in half with a sharp knife.

3 Drain; discard the soaking water.

4 Place 4 cups of fresh water and the soaked beans in a 2-quart saucepan and bring to a boil (do not add salt until after the beans are cooked). Reduce the heat and simmer, partially covered, for the suggested cooking time given below. (Start checking for doneness at the earlier cooking time.)

BEAN COOKING TABLE

TYPE OF BEAN	COOKING TIME
Black	1 to 1 1/2 hrs.
Black-eyed peas	3/4 to 1 1/2 hrs.
Cannellini	1 to 1 1/2 hrs.
Chickpeas	2 to 3 hrs.
Great Northern	1 to 2 hrs.
Kidney	1 to 2 hrs.
Lentils	1/2 to 1 hr.
Lima (baby)	3/4 to 1 1/2 hrs.
Lima (large)	1 to 1 1/2 hrs.
Navy (small white)	1 to 2 hrs.
Pink	1 to 2 hrs.
Pinto	1 to 2 hrs.
Roman (cranberry)	1 to 2 hrs.
Soy	2 1/2 to 3 1/2 hrs.

COOKING BASICS

MAIL-ORDER SOURCES

BOB'S RED MILL NATURAL FOODS

5209 SE International Way
Milwaukee, OK 97222
(800) 349-2173
(503) 653-1339 (fax)
www.bobredmill.com

—Primarily grains, some beans

DEAN & DELUCA

560 Broadway
New York, NY 11101
www.deandeluca.com

—Gourmet foods, grains, beans, coffees, equipment, books

EDEN FOODS

701 Tecumseh Road
Clinton, MI 49236
(800) 424-3336
www.edenfoods.com

—Beans, grains, syrups, large variety of products

THE VEGAN STORE

2381 Lewis Avenue
Rockville, MD 20851
(800) 340 -1200
www.veganstore.com

—Textured vegetable protein (TVP), vegetable burgers, all kinds of vegan products

INDEX